"Clear, concise, informative, witty and, believe it or not, entertaining.... We are grateful that in addressing such a complex and difficult subject, Wheelan provides in full measure three of the rarest and most highly desired qualities of good writing: illumination, pleasure and clarity."

—E. William Smethurst Jr., *Chicago Tribune*

"Bravo, Charles Wheelan, for doing the impossible: making the study of economics fascinating, comprehensible, and laugh-out-loud funny." —Deborah Copaken Kogan, author of *Shutterbabe: Adventures in Love and War*

Naked Statistics

"Sparkling and intensely readable.... A great measure of the book's appeal comes from Mr. Wheelan's fluent style—a natural comedian, he is truly the Dave Barry of the coin toss set."

—Abigail Zuger, *New York Times Book Review*

"[Wheelan] does something unique here: he makes statistics interesting and fun. His book strips the subject of its complexity to expose the sexy stuff underneath." —*The Economist*

We Came, We Saw, We Left

"Engaging, insightful, and downright pleasant."

—Nathan Deuel, *Los Angeles Times*

"Wheelan is a lucid and likable storyteller, and his antic family dialogues are spot-on. . . . [A]n upbeat story."

—Amity Gaige, *New York Times Book Review*

WRITE
FOR YOUR
LIFE

WRITE
FOR YOUR
LIFE

A Guide to Clear and

Purposeful Writing

(and Presentations)

CHARLES WHEELAN

W. W. NORTON & COMPANY
Celebrating a Century of Independent Publishing

For information about permission to reproduce selections from this book, write to
Permissions, W. W. Norton & Company, Inc., 500 Fifth Avenue, New York, NY 10110

For information about special discounts for bulk purchases, please contact
W. W. Norton Special Sales at specialsales@wwnorton.com or 800-233-4830

Manufacturing by Lakeside Book Company
Book design by Chris Welch
Production manager: Devon Zahn

Library of Congress Cataloging-in-Publication Data

Names: Wheelan, Charles J., author.
Title: Write for your life : a guide to clear and purposeful writing (and presentations) /
Charles Wheelan.
Description: First edition. | New York, NY : W. W. Norton & Company, 2022. |
Includes bibliographical references.
Identifiers: LCCN 2021062329 | ISBN 9780393633979 (hardcover) |
ISBN 9780393633986 (epub)
Subjects: LCSH: Business writing—Handbooks, manuals, etc. |
Rhetoric—Handbooks, manuals, etc. | Oratory—Handbooks, manuals, etc.
Classification: LCC HF5718.3 .W53 2022 | DDC 808.06/665—dc23/eng/20220112
LC record available at https://lccn.loc.gov/2021062329

ISBN 978-1-324-06446-6 pbk.

W. W. Norton & Company, Inc.
500 Fifth Avenue, New York, N.Y. 10110
www.wwnorton.com

W. W. Norton & Company Ltd.
15 Carlisle Street, London W1D 3BS

1 2 3 4 5 6 7 8 9 0

For my teachers

Contents

HOW LOST IS HE?

About a decade ago, I went skiing in Colorado with my family. I was entrusted for the day with my nephew, Nate, who was eight years old at the time. After lunch, Nate asked if he could ski on his own, which seemed like a reasonable request. I pointed to a pine tree near one of the chairlifts. "Meet me under that tree at four o'clock," I instructed. Nate skied off to the lift line.

At four o'clock, I returned to our designated rendezvous point. Nate was not waiting by the pine tree. Fifteen minutes later, he still had not returned. I was mildly concerned: *had I lost someone else's child?* More minutes went by, and Nate still had not turned up. Now I was worried enough that I decided to report Nate missing to the Ski Patrol. If something terrible had happened—if Nate had broken his leg and been airlifted to a Denver hospital—the Ski Patrol would know.

I found the Ski Patrol office, where a man behind a desk

appeared to be wrapping up work for the day. "How can I help you?" he asked.

"I've lost a child," I said.

The man sized me up for a moment and then asked, "How lost is he?"

Technically, that phrase is ungrammatical. Lost is a binary condition; something is either lost or not lost. Nothing can be "more lost" or "less lost." Either I knew where Nate was, or I did not.

In this moment, as I stood plaintively in front of the Ski Patrol officer, I did *not* know where Nate was. Yet the Ski Patrolman's question—"How lost is he?"—was a brilliant use of language. With just four words, this gentleman told me a number of things. First, he signaled that Nate was not seriously hurt. If there were an injured child lying on a cot in the Ski Patrol center, the Ski Patrolman would have asked me, "What's his name?"

Or, if Nate were so seriously hurt that he was unconscious as they airlifted him to Denver, the Ski Patrolman might have asked, "Is he a boy with dark hair and a blue coat who looks to be about eight years old?"

This gentleman did not ask any of those things. Instead, his question—just four words—suggested something more reassuring: young people get lost every day at a ski resort and they get lost in different kinds of ways. There is "lost" when two men jump out of a white van, nab a child, and race away, tires screeching. That kind of incident is rare, bordering on nonexistent. And there is "lost" when a young, semiresponsible boy who might be tempted to take an extra run does not show up at the appointed time. As I reflected on the question, I knew Nate was the second kind of lost. I was not processing these thoughts consciously; rather, they were racing through my mind subconsciously, which was the genius of the question: "How lost is he?"

I answered, "Not very lost."

The Ski Patrolman nodded in a friendly, unconcerned way. "Why don't you go back to where you said you'd meet him and see if he's there," he advised.

I walked back to the pine tree, where Nate was waiting patiently for me.

Language is how we interact with other humans. Words matter. Politicians use language to sell their ideas and capabilities. *Hope and Change.* With just three words, Barack Obama embodied the promise of his presidency. *Make America Great Again* did the same thing for Donald Trump. That's four words, and I suspect you responded to them with strong emotion.

Journalists write to inform us as succinctly and accurately as possible. Columnists write to persuade us, or to inspire us to think in new ways. Comedians spend months or years crafting a joke. One misplaced word and the joke falls flat. Entrepreneurs write business plans to attract investors. Dave Girouard, former president of Google Apps and the founder and CEO of Upstart, feels so strongly about the importance of good writing in business that he wrote a manifesto, *A Founder's Guide to Writing Well*. He declared, "Of the many skills attributed to successful entrepreneurs—vision, execution, persuasion, perseverance, grit, resilience—effective writing inevitably fails to make the list. Yet I submit to you that the quality of your writing contributes to the outcomes you experience as a founder and executive day in and day out."[1]

Judges use language to render decisions. There is a winner and a loser in every case, but those verdicts also provide guidance for other courts. When the Supreme Court renders a decision, such as a verdict on the role of affirmative action in college admissions, the language in the majority opinion is an instruction manual for the lower courts. The clearer the language, the less confusion there will be around that legal issue in future decades.

Sloppy writing sows confusion. The Second Amendment to the US Constitution reads: "A well regulated Militia, being necessary to the security of a free State, the right of the people to keep and bear Arms, shall not be infringed." I have great admiration for the Constitution, but that sentence was not the framers' best work. What exactly does that cumbersome, passive sentence tell us about whether Washington, D.C., can ban handguns? Legal scholars and policymakers have been arguing about the meaning of the Second Amendment for as long as I have been alive.

When President George W. Bush nominated White House Counsel Harriet Miers to serve on the Supreme Court in 2005, *New York Times* columnist David Brooks wrote a scathing appraisal of her qualification to serve on the high court. His complaint was not based on Miers's ideology or her legal experience. He objected to her abysmally poor writing, which he believed indicated a lack of clear thinking. Brooks cited passages like this one: "We have to understand and appreciate that achieving justice for all is in jeopardy before a call to arms to assist in obtaining support for the justice system will be effective. Achieving the necessary understanding and appreciation of why the challenge is so important, we can then turn to the task of providing the much needed support."[2]

It is hard to finish those sentences without skimming; I've read them repeatedly and I still have no idea what they mean. Brooks, a wonderful columnist, wrote, "Surely the threshold skill required of a Supreme Court justice is the ability to write clearly and argue incisively. Miers's columns provide no evidence of that." President George W. Bush ultimately withdrew the Miers nomination. There were a lot of reasons for that, but the trail of opaque legal writing did not help.

What does great legal writing look like? Elena Kagan is the best writer on the current Supreme Court, says Jennifer Sargent, a colleague of mine at Dartmouth College who teaches legal writing. "Kagan is the most persuasive writer, and that's the job of a jurist," Sargent explains. Justice Kagan has an aptitude for writing majority opinions, which require language that can hold a coalition of justices together, like a diplomat finding common ground and avoiding points of disagreement.[3] But Elena Kagan's dissents are where her writing soars. Dissenting opinions are written by justices in the minority—the losers in a particular case. These opinions are less constrained because there is no need to hold together a coalition. They are meant to find fault with the majority decision, often with an eye to history. "Like good journalism, the best dissents are often colloquial, as if the writer were telling a story about the case to friends over dinner," says Jeffrey Rosen, the legal editor of the *New Republic*.[4]

Elena Kagan's writing is not brilliant because she uses fancy words and makes esoteric historical references. Rather, she uses the tools that will be described in this book: clear, straightforward language; a coherent narrative structure; rigorous editing; and even humor if it serves to make a point. Justice Kagan cited Dr. Seuss (*One Fish Two Fish Red Fish Blue Fish*) in a 2015 case involving illegal fishing.[5] She is one of only two justices in the history of the court to use the word "chutzpah" in an opinion. (Antonin Scalia, another great legal writer, was the first.)[6]

Ironically, great writing can be deliberately opaque. Former US senator George Mitchell played a crucial role in negotiating the agreement that ended the violent conflict between Protestants and Catholics in Northern Ireland, the Good Friday Agreement. Mitchell wrote in his memoir that vague language was essential to getting the final agreement approved. The parties had been at war for so long, and the various constituencies had developed such hardened positions, that no agreement was possible "unless the language was sufficiently elastic to allow it to be read differently by opposing sides."[7] The murky language in the Good Friday Agreement became known as "constructive ambiguity." The prose was so convoluted in places that it spawned a joke: "What do you get if you cross the Northern Ireland peace process with the mafia?" Answer: "An offer you can't refuse and can't understand."

Writing is how we give directions, file criminal complaints, compose love letters, report the news, pitch investment ideas, complain to our landlords, and undertake most other important life endeavors. Language is the code of life; writing is how we make that code clear and effective. Bad writing is like bad computer code: it obscures, confuses, and works against what we are trying to accomplish (unless unclear writing is essential to what we are trying to accomplish).

The spoken word matters, too. Franklin Roosevelt used language to assuage Americans' fears during the Great Depression. His medium was radio; the tool was succinct, powerful, and inspiring language. Writing and speaking are two sides of the same coin; they both require using language to good effect. I have been involved with that coin in various ways for my entire career. Twice I have worked as a speechwriter, first for the governor of Maine and later for former Chicago mayor Richard M. Daley. Writing is always hard; putting words in someone else's mouth is uniquely stressful. I recall a particularly scathing critique by the governor as he reviewed the draft of a speech. "Is this supposed to be funny?" he asked angrily. *"Because if it is, it isn't."* His word choice was clever, albeit devastating to me in that moment.

I worked for five years as the Midwest correspondent for *The Economist*, a British weekly news magazine. My job was to report on topics across the American Midwest and produce succinct stories, rarely more than a thousand words. Years later, I ran for Congress in Chicago during the depths of the financial crisis. I gave speech after speech explaining what I stood for as a candidate and why I ought to be elected. (I wasn't.) I have worked as a columnist, using analysis and data and humor to try to explain complex topics like health care and tax policy, and I have written books on economics and statistics and monetary policy. I don't know more about those topics than other academics; I have been able to write about them in ways that make them understandable and even enjoyable for lay readers.

For all that, what motivated me to write this book is my teaching. For nearly twenty years, I have taught public policy to graduate students and undergraduates, first at the University of Chicago and now at Dartmouth College. My students are invariably bright and motivated; however, many of them do not write well enough to thrive in a professional setting. This should not be a great surprise. Most writing assignments in school are, by necessity, somewhat artificial: reports, essays, and term papers. That is not writing for the real world. Most people do not make a living by writing ten pages on whales or by describing the symbolism in *Paradise Lost* (with the obvious exception of nature writers and book reviewers).

Writing for life is different. It requires composing your thoughts in a way that gets your desired response, whether that is laughs in a comedy club, a raise from your boss, a large donation to a food pantry, or something else. This is a crucial life skill. As Upstart CEO Dave Girouard points out in his manifesto, "Poor writing can harm you in so many ways: logic is hidden, points are lost, news is buried, intent is misread, feelings are hurt, credibility suffers. And that assumes anybody actually reads what you wrote." Remember, he's not an English teacher; he runs companies for a living.

What kind of writing for life might you do? You might start a company, as Dave Girouard did with Upstart. How cool would it be to design crucial software for a self-driving car or to engineer a medical device that makes surgery safer and more effective? Here is how you would get started: *by writing your business plan.* Long before your product gets to market, you will need to raise millions of dollars to fund your startup. You cannot do that by inviting investors to your parents' basement and exclaiming, "Bro, you have no idea how awesome this idea is!" Rather, you will write a business plan that explains to investors in explicit detail how your product will work, how it will be different from related products on the market, who will buy it, how much they will pay, and, most important, what kind of return your investors will make if all goes as planned (and how much they will lose if it doesn't). The most prominent venture capital firms get about a hundred business plans for every one they invest in. You might be thinking: *The ideas that get passed up must be lousy.* We don't know that. What we know is that the ideas that get passed up are not compelling *as described in the business plan.*

You might have some modest suggestion for how the world could be made better: a new crosswalk near your home; a change in zoning laws; legislation to improve policing. How do you set those changes in motion? You write to the officials who are in a position to authorize or vote on them. Your letter or email will be stacked with hundreds of other ideas that range from sensible to insane. To move your idea to the top of that pile, you may circulate a petition or write an opinion piece for the local newspaper (both of which will require clear, succinct, compelling language). All political and social change is rooted in effective communication, from small projects at the local level to decades-long national movements. When Martin Luther King Jr. was arrested in Birmingham, Alabama, in 1963, he wrote the Letter from Birmingham Jail. This was not a long complaint about the food. It was a letter to explain the purpose and value of his nonviolent civil disobedience campaign, particularly to white clergy who had been critical of his efforts. The letter is compelling enough that it was published as a pamphlet, reprinted in publications like *Ebony* and the *New York Post*, and introduced as testimony in the US House of Representatives.[8]

In 1995, Hillary Clinton gave a speech in Beijing at a United Nations conference on Women in which she famously declared, "Women's rights are human rights, and human rights are women's rights."[9] As I will discuss later, the speech was much more than one powerful line, but the overall effect was to reframe the way women's rights are perceived around the globe. "It was Hillary Clinton's declaration that jump started a global movement," says Allida Black, a historian and founding editor of the Eleanor Roosevelt Papers Project.

Okay, you may not lead a social movement, and one hopes you won't be incarcerated in Alabama. But you are likely to have a job of some sort. Every facet of that work will require clarity of communication: with your customers; with your coworkers; with your boss.

For ideas big and small, the quality of your writing will signal your clarity of thought. Harriet Miers is not currently on the Supreme Court; Elena Kagan is.

Your writing will sell others on your plans: Dave Girouard's company Upstart went public in 2020 and was valued at roughly $1.5 billion.

And writing will play a crucial role in your overall success. The white clergy on the receiving end of Martin Luther King's letter from jail became an important source of support in the larger civil rights movement.

Whatever you do, good writing will help.

Years ago, I began keeping an ad hoc list of writing suggestions that I distributed to my students each term. At first, the list was ten suggestions on one page. Over time, the list grew. These were not tips for better grammar or beautiful prose. They were suggestions for *effective writing*: clear, succinct, compelling, and, most important, appropriate to the task at hand. That list eventually became this book.

Meanwhile, I observed that leaders across a range of fields tend to be proficient in public speaking. The women and men who inhabit positions of respect and authority speak cogently and clearly. They are organized and credible. They can speak to a meeting or a large group in a way that projects competence. In some ways, that is what defines leadership: an ability to use words to motivate, to persuade, to soothe. Britain's Queen Elizabeth II had a speech prepared in the early 1980s to be delivered if a Soviet attack precipitated World War III. ("But whatever terrors lie in wait for us, all the qualities that have helped to keep our freedom intact twice already during this sad century will once more be our strength.")[10] Thankfully, that one never came out of the drawer.

Speaking for life is important, too. Of course, solid public speaking is not radically different from good writing. You organize words to good effect—and then say them out loud. In fact, the boundary between writing and presenting is more fluid than one might think. When the president of the United States gives his State of the Union Address, the remarks are prepared in advance and then delivered before Congress and the nation. If one reads prepared remarks from a teleprompter, is that a written document or a presentation? For the purposes of this book, who cares?

At Amazon, founder Jeff Bezos discouraged PowerPoint presentations. His successor Andy Jassy asks each presenter to compose a six-page memo, which may take up to a week to prepare and is distributed to meeting attendees in advance. The meeting is then spent discussing the memo. Would you describe that process as writing a memo, making a presentation, or both? Again, for purposes of this book, it is a distinction without a difference. The intersection between good writing and effective presentations is clear and compelling communication.

Consider one example of how important communication is to success. On August 9, 1940, Winston Churchill sent a memo to his cabinet. This was a low point in World War II for the United Kingdom. Britain was facing nightly bombings from the German Luftwaffe. France had collapsed and signed an armistice with Nazi Germany. The United States had not yet entered the war. At a time that Churchill described as "the darkest hour," what did he demand from his war cabinet?

Better writing.

The first sentences of Churchill's 1940 memo to the cabinet implored, "To do our work, we all have to read a mass of papers. Nearly all of them are far too long. This wastes time, while energy has to be spent looking for the essential points." Winning the war would require (among other things) shorter, clearer memos. Meanwhile, Churchill used his remarkable verbal ability to give radio addresses that rallied the nation.

Even if the fate of a nation is not in your hands, writing and speaking effectively are crucial professional skills. Can you communicate in ways that inform, inspire, and motivate? Can you articulate your ideas so that they lead to the intended outcome, whether that is getting a public toilet fixed or ending a violent conflict?

That is writing (and speaking) for your life.

WRITE
FOR YOUR
LIFE

GETTING STARTED

1. Why are you writing this?

The first step to good writing is determining
what you expect it to accomplish.

Let's start at the beginning. You are sitting at the keyboard, or perhaps in front of a blank piece of paper. You intend to write something.

Why?

Doesn't that seem like a reasonable question? If you were to stop at a gas station and ask for directions, the attendant would ask where you are trying to go. If you cannot answer that question, even the most helpful person cannot offer directions. Or, to use a more technologically sophisticated example, a state-of-the-art navigational system will not give you turn-by-turn directions until you enter a destination.

So it is with writing. We cannot define "good writing" until we know the point of it. Are you trying to thank Grandma for the Amazon gift card? If so, then good writing will be a succinct, handwritten note that makes specific mention of why you appreciated the gift. Making it heartfelt and sending it promptly will count more than anything else. If Grandma is pleased when she reads your card, you are Shakespeare in that moment.

A reporter once asked Major League pitcher Greg Maddux how fast he threw his fastball. Maddux replied tartly, "Fast enough." Maddux was annoyed by the question because he was needled throughout his career for not pitching the ball particularly hard, even his fastball. Here is the beauty of Maddux's curt response to the reporter: It called out the fallacy of the question. *The point of pitching is not to throw the ball hard. The point is to get batters out.* Sure, throwing fast can help, but if a batter swings and misses at a slow pitch that bounces twice before reaching the plate, it's still a strike. Maddux won three hundred and fifty-five games in his twenty-three-year career. He is one of only ten pitchers in history to win three hundred games and to get three thousand strikeouts. He was the first pitcher in major league history to win the Cy Young Award (best pitcher in baseball) four years in a row. He was inducted into the Baseball Hall of Fame in 2014.

Fast enough.

The same is true with writing. Unless you are writing poetry or literary fiction, the purpose of writing is not to create beautiful sentences with lyrical language and elegant metaphors. *The purpose of writing is to accomplish something.*

What words (and images) will inspire people to write a check, to march in the street, to elect a particular politician, or to respond in some other meaningful way? The measure of your prose is not how elegantly you describe melting polar ice caps. It is whether what you have written inspires people to do something about climate change, recognizing that a devastating description of melting polar ice caps might help in that regard.

This is not how most of us learned to write in school. Why did we write a six-page paper on cockroaches in Mrs. Thompson's English class? Because it counted for 30 percent of the semester grade. Why did Mrs. Thompson read those papers? Because she was paid to read them. She would get fired if she didn't (or at least if she got caught not reading them and did not have tenure). College brings longer papers on more esoteric topics. The basic exercise is still the same: Write a paper to fulfill an assignment for a professor whose job it is to read what you have written. This is not a book about writing better term papers. It's about writing for what comes after that.

Once you are out of school, no one is going to get fired for not finishing your irrelevant or overly long memos. In fact, if you consistently produce things that no one wants to read, you're the one who will get fired. If you write poetic campaign speeches for candidates who lose, your career in politics will be short. If you write brilliant jokes that audiences don't laugh at, your time on stage at comedy clubs will be short and probably very uncomfortable, too.

Hillary Clinton's influential 1995 speech on women's

rights began with a clear purpose. On the flight to the conference in Beijing, as Clinton worked on successive drafts, Madeleine Albright, US ambassador to the United Nations (and later secretary of state) asked her, "What do you want to accomplish?"

"I want to push the envelope as far as I can on behalf of women and children," Clinton replied.[1] That is what she did. American Rhetoric judged her speech in Beijing to be one of the most significant political speeches of the twentieth century.[2]

Having disparaged poetry a few paragraphs back, I should point out that Hillary Clinton's decision to speak out about women's rights was motivated in part by a young student's poem that she had heard at a different conference:

Too many women,
In too many countries
Speak the same language,
Of silence.[3]

"I couldn't get the poem out of my head," Hillary Clinton said. In the right place at the right time, poetry can change the world, too.

The architect Louis Sullivan, pioneer of the modern skyscraper, believed that "form should follow function." Great architecture produces a building that is well suited for its purpose. Writing is the same. Why are you sitting in front of your computer? Do you want to make people laugh? Are you urging the boss to fire the annoying guy who works in the carrel next to you? Do you need to raise a million dollars to build a municipal swimming pool?

Start with why. Then move to how.

2. Know your audience.

*Your writing should be catered to
those for whom it is intended.*

Good writers think about their readers. Suppose you are writing a public letter expressing safety concerns about a proposed nuclear power plant. Who is going to read this letter? Are you writing it for the nuclear scientists designing the plant? Or are you writing it for the people who own houses near the proposed site? Because those are two very different groups. One will care a lot about isotopes (I'm guessing here), and the other will care about property values (I'm more certain of that). Writing something without an audience in mind is like firing a weapon without a target.

My mother once returned from a speech by a famous economist and lamented, "I didn't understand it. I'm not smart enough." *Wrong.* The only dumb person involved in that speech was the person giving it, who didn't take the time to think about her audience. She was accustomed to speaking to other academics and did not adapt her talk for a group of smart laypeople.

I once did something similar, by accident. I was giving a

talk on health care in Canada, and my goal was to make a distinction between health care policies that are top-notch and those that are decent but not optimal. I settled on an analogy familiar to every American who has gone to high school: the varsity team and junior varsity team (or JV). The example felt clever to me: Varsity is best; JV is not so good. I went through my speech, making frequent references to varsity and JV. After I was done, a member of the Canadian audience came up to me and asked, "What is JV?" Whoops.

Great writers and speakers *begin* by thinking about their audience. Sports columnists write for those who are passionate about sports. It would be ridiculous for a *Chicago Sun-Times* sportswriter to remind his readers that in football, each touchdown is worth six points. On the other hand, a British columnist attempting to explain American football to readers in London would be remiss if he did not point out that fact. He would then have to explain the arcane process of deciding between kicking for an extra point or trying to advance the ball into the end zone again for two points.

I recall seeing an aphorism posted on the wall of a Chicago Public Radio studio: "Never overestimate how much the listeners know about a specific subject, but never underestimate how intelligent they are." That admonition framed the challenge for anyone speaking to a public radio audience. Do not rely on technical jargon to make a point. Parents listening to the radio while dropping their kids off at school are not going to understand terms like "elasticity of labor supply." If a guest relies on that kind of technical language, listeners across the Chicago area will change the station to easy listening or sports talk. Yet the second half of that admonition is a reminder that public radio listeners are smart, thoughtful people interested in complex subjects. Don't patronize them, and don't avoid complicated subjects. Rather, be mindful of broaching those topics with sufficient background that the listener can get a foothold in the conversation.

When I have students write policy memos for class, I typically have them address their memos to a particular person, like the governor of New Jersey or a senior staff member for the Joint Committee on Taxation. Obviously, these individuals will never see the student memos. Rather, the simple exercise of addressing the memo to a real person reminds the students of the target audience. If it is the governor of New Jersey, they do not need to explain how a bill becomes a law. However, they may need to explain technical terms related to the topic. The governor, however smart, is a generalist, not an expert. On the other hand, the staff of the Joint Committee on Taxation are likely to be experts in economics and tax law. They will understand terms like "elasticity" and "externality" and "substitution effect." Using technical language for this audience will make the memo shorter and clearer. In fact, these readers may be bored or insulted if the memo is overly basic, just as the governor would be annoyed if the memo explained how a bill becomes a law.

As your parents may have advised you, think about other

people. Specifically, who will be reading what you write? How much or how little do they know about the subject? How much detail do they need? How much time do they have? Why do they have an interest in the subject? What information will make their jobs easier?

Yes, your name will be on this document. You are the writer. *But what's in it for the reader?*

3. Sometimes there is more than one audience.

You may need multiple documents to address different stakeholders.

If you are struggling to craft a single document that resonates with audiences who do not speak the same language—literally or figuratively—the solution may lie in producing something for each of them. This does not change the "why" of what you are trying to achieve, but different groups may need different routes to get to the same destination. Marketers routinely use different advertisements for different audiences, just as politicians adapt their messages depending on who is listening. There is nothing insidious about this. Business and policy types refer to this process as stakeholder analysis. Stakeholders are people and groups that have overlapping but not identical interests. The key to effective communication is addressing each group's primary interests. If you are having trouble writing something because there are too many ideas pulling you in different directions, the problem may be foundational: *this is not meant to be one document.* If you will be giving presentations to these different groups, do not recycle the exact same slides and jokes. Speak to the audience sitting in front of you.

I was hired in 2002 by a civic group in Chicago that was advocating for more coherent regional policies related to housing, taxes, transportation, and education. The group, Chicago Metropolis 2020, had hired a consultant who produced a highly technical report in support of these policies. It was excellent work ... and four hundred pages long. I was hired in part to rewrite the report so that it would be a more effective tool for promoting our ideas to local opinion leaders, such as mayors and journalists. "It needs to be shorter and punchier," my new boss told me.

My first insight was that there was no "it." The consultant had given us valuable work, but if I tried to condense four hundred pages into two hundred pages, or even a hundred pages, I was still going to have something that was longer and denser than most people could absorb. Most readers wanted much, much less. I wrote a thirty-six-page report summarizing the technical work in a way that was accessible for lay readers. We added graphics and charts to make it more visually interesting. Meanwhile, we kept the original report since there were some people, such as the engineering staff at the Illinois Department of Transportation, who were interested in seeing all the data: the models, the assumptions, the various scenarios. These people would want to "look under the hood" at the models; we ought to offer them everything we had.

Now we had the best of all worlds: a more succinct document that would spare readers from having to wade into the weeds, but also a longer document for those so inclined to plunge in. But there was more work to do. One member of our staff was related to the mayor of Chicago. She told us that the mayor was interested in our ideas but would never have time to read a thirty-six-page report. She suggested that we produce a trifold document—six pages overall—summarizing our key findings and recommendations. We hired a designer who integrated lovely aerial photos of Chicago and colorful illustrations that we commissioned for the project. Anyone who saw the trifold would be tempted to pick it up and page through it—which is the opposite of most dense policy memos. It was also short enough, and cheap enough to print, that we could pass it out when we did presentations.

Still, I was not done. We began lobbying the Illinois General Assembly to adopt our policy recommendations as law.* A former elected official warned us that when the legislature was in session, legislators did not have time to read six pages. She suggested that I write a "one-pager"—a single page encapsulating the essence of what we were trying to do and what legislative "asks" were required. I wrote a one-page document summarizing the key elements of our work.

Remarkably, we needed something even shorter than the

---

* One of those state legislators was State Senator Barack Obama.

one-pager. My boss was scheduled to ride in a car with the governor of Illinois, giving them fifteen minutes together. This was a unique opportunity to pitch our legislative ideas to the guy who would have to sign the bills. That guy was Rod Blagojevich, who would later be convicted and imprisoned for trying to sell Barack Obama's Senate seat. (He burst back into the news when President Donald Trump commuted his prison sentence.) At the time, however, Governor Blagojevich was just an elected official with relatively little interest in policy and a short attention span. "I need three bullet points," my boss told me. The one-pager was too long for Governor Blagojevich. I dutifully composed three bullet points that encapsulated what we were trying to do and why we were trying to do it.

To recap: we turned a four-hundred-page report into a thirty-six-page summary that became a six-page flier and then a one-pager and finally a mere three bullet points. Each of those documents served its purpose for a particular audience. It would have been ludicrous to explain our plans to traffic engineers using three bullet points. It would have been equally absurd to give Governor Blagojevich the four-hundred-page report. In the end, we did a lot of thoughtful writing and delivered a consistent message to different constituencies.

Remember, your objective is not to create a single document with beautiful prose. Your objective is whatever you identified in #1. If that requires multiple documents because engineers love data, state legislators are busy, and the governor has a short attention span, so be it.

4. Good writing begins with a clear thesis.

The thesis is a succinct articulation of the point or points you are trying to make.

You have determined *why* you are sitting in front of the computer, and you have considered *who* will be reading what you write. Now we have arrived at *what*. What is the essential idea that you want your readers to absorb? Before your fingers hit the keyboard, you should be able to encapsulate what you plan to write in one sentence. The balance of what you write will explain and defend this core idea, which is your thesis. Here are some examples:

> We need more diversity in the economics department.
> People over sixty-five should get a shingles vaccination.
> The court should issue a warrant to search the property because we have compelling evidence that there is a meth lab in the basement.
> A man your age should not be wearing white skinny jeans.[*]

The thesis—the what—typically follows from the why, just as form follows function in architecture. Suppose you have just graduated from high school and are living in a one-bedroom

---

[*] This is a real example drawn from an email I sent to a high school friend.

apartment with seven friends. There is a strange smell coming from the basement that the landlord has refused to deal with. Your roommates assign you (the only person in the group who has read this book) to write an email to the landlord demanding that she fix the smell or reduce your rent by $200. The thesis of that note is straightforward: *Fix this unpleasant odor or give us a $200 break in the rent as compensation for enduring it.* The balance of the email should substantiate the thesis.

- Describe the smell.
- Document the landlord's failure to address the smell.
- Explain why a $200 reduction in the rent is appropriate compensation for enduring the smell if it is not remediated.

Any thoughts and ideas that do not support the thesis should be left out. Perhaps it is annoying that the landlord parks her truck in your driveway when she visits a neighboring unit, but that is not why you are writing the letter. Extraneous items will detract from your core message: *Fix the smell or knock $200 off the rent.* That's the point here. Leave the parking complaint for another email.

Bear in mind the old aphorism, "If you have too many priorities, you have none." When writers go off track, it is often because a document lacks focus or purpose. The idea of a thesis sentence has been bastardized by decades of bad school essays: "Spiders are arachnids" and "The Sumerians were an important early civilization." These thesis statements feel superfluous because the writing projects themselves are superfluous. The good news is that when you write for life, the thesis will feel more relevant and obvious because it matters. *I am qualified to be an intern at your cybersecurity firm* (cover letter). *Our muffins are losing market share to our competitors because we do not have a resealable package* (email to the brand manager). *Please stop letting your dog poop on our lawn* (letter slipped under the neighbor's door). Your thesis should feel helpful, even liberating, because it is a writing North Star for focusing your document. Things that support the thesis go in; things that don't support the thesis come out.

If you are giving a presentation, you should be able to say at the outset: "I am here today to tell you/persuade you/explain to you _____." What? You should be able to finish that sentence. If you cannot, lots of slides with pictures of cute animals will not rescue your talk.

A clever thesis can unify seemingly disparate ideas. Imagine a commencement speaker who begins his address with a series of random statements: "Make sure you take as much toilet paper as your parents will give you. Eating ramen noodles five nights a week will not harm your long-term health. Find a roommate with a Netflix account." At this point in the speech, the president of the university will shift uncomfortably in her seat. Parents will whisper, "We paid tens of thousands of dollars in tuition *for this*?" Students will text one another speculating about whether or not the speaker is drunk.

Yet these random observations could be unified with a simple thesis, just one sentence at the beginning of the speech: *Here are ten things I learned in the year after my graduation.* Now those disparate lessons make sense. Their randomness becomes a source of humor because the thesis has given them context.

A long, complicated document will have an overarching thesis: the big idea. Each section or chapter will have its own thesis that supports the larger mission of the document. Consider a new police superintendent who is producing a report on his plan to improve police relations with the community. The introduction to the report will present the thesis: *Police relations with the community need to improve, and I have a plan for making that happen.* Each subsequent section of the report, whether it is a paragraph or a chapter, will have a thesis of its own:

- Police-community relations have deteriorated to a degree that is not acceptable.
- Poor police-community relations lead to less effective law enforcement.
- The primary problem is a lack of trust between officers and civilians, particularly people of color.
- I have three major initiatives to improve trust.
- These kinds of programs have worked in other cities like ours and will likely be successful here, too.
- My tenure as superintendent should be judged on my success in improving police-community relations.

Each bullet point is a discrete idea that can be more fully developed. Each is also supportive of the overarching thesis of the document. Together, they build a case for why police–community relations need to improve and how it will happen. The *why, who,* and *what* of this document are clear.

Why is the police superintendent writing it? *To restore faith in the police force.*

Who is the intended audience? *Members of the community.*

What is the big idea in the report? *Our police department needs to interact more effectively with the community, and we can make that happen.*

When Churchill sent the memo to his cabinet demanding better writing, his thesis was clear: "I ask my colleagues and their staffs to see to it that their Reports are shorter." He then offered four specific suggestions for achieving that. (The full memo can be found in Appendix A.)

Your thesis should explain—to you and to others—why you are sitting in front of the keyboard (or standing at the front of the room). If you cannot encapsulate what you plan to write in one clear sentence, do not start typing. Once you are comfortable with the thesis—if you can explain to your mother or your roommate or your mail carrier what you plan to write in one clear sentence—then you can begin to think about how best to defend and explain that thesis.

5. Organize your thoughts into a coherent narrative structure.

*Your organizational structure is how
you choose to tell your story.*

No typing yet.

Yes, you have decided *why* you are writing something and *for whom* you are writing it. And yes, you have formulated a thesis. You know the overarching point that you are trying to make. But you still have not decided *how* you will present your case to the reader. This is perhaps the most underappreciated challenge of writing: *there are an infinite number of ways to tell any story.* Think about successful films and novels. Sometimes a story begins at the end. In the first scene, a group of people stare at a dead body, and then the story jumps back in time (e.g., "FIVE YEARS EARLIER") to explain how that person ended up dead. The film *The Hangover* famously begins with four men stranded in the desert. We know only that one of them, Doug, is about to get married. One of the guys, who is bleeding from his mouth, makes a call to the prospective bride. "The bachelor party ... the whole night ... things got out of control, and we lost Doug," he says.

"We're getting married in five hours!" the bride exclaims.

The guy says, "Yeah, that's not gonna happen."

The film then cuts back to two days earlier to tell the story of how those characters end up stranded in the desert.

The classic film *Rashomon* (based on a short story of the

same name) tells one story over and over, but each time the story is told from the perspective of a new character who recalls the events differently. The enduring point of the film is that "reality" can be described in many ways.

Imagine a trial lawyer preparing her closing arguments in a case against a corporate polluter. The why of this exercise is clear: *win the case.*

The audience—the who—is obvious: *the twelve members of the jury.*

The lawyer's thesis is straightforward, too: *the company acted negligently and did grave harm to my client.*

But how should this case be presented to the jury? The lawyer can illustrate the polluting firm's negligent behavior in innumerable ways. She could begin by describing repeated acts of malfeasance: the corporate officers who ignored reports that the town drinking water was orange; the scientists fired for drawing attention to the three-headed snakes discovered on the school playground; the CEO who refused to drink tap water in the executive dining room; and so on. Then, after describing this litany of corporate malfeasance, the lawyer would ask dramatically: *And what was the effect of all this negligent behavior?* At that point, she would introduce the victims.

The lawyer could make the same point in reverse. She could introduce the victims, describing their horrible illnesses, and then ask: *How did this happen?* Then she would present the examples of corporate malfeasance.

Or she could impose some arbitrary organizational tool on

her remarks: "Here are five things you need to understand about this company's negligent behavior as you head into the jury room."

Each of these narrative structures could work to successfully defend the thesis: *This company did bad things that harmed my clients.* I am not a lawyer, so I have no idea which approach would work best. What I do know is that the lawyer cannot just begin speaking without organizing her thoughts, even if she knows exactly what points the jury needs to hear. She needs an effective structure for organizing her story.

Remember Justice Elena Kagan, the best writer on the current Supreme Court? One element of her great writing is a clear organizational structure. In a profile of Justice Kagan in *The New Yorker*, Margaret Talbot writes, "Kagan's gifts as a writer have less to do with vivid turns of phrase than with the ability to maintain readers' attention, guiding them from argument to argument, with the implicit assurance that they will encounter a beginning, a middle, and an end."[4]

The need for a narrative structure helps to explain why staring at a blank page can be torturous, even if you know exactly what you want to say. Writing is not like math, where there is typically a process for working your way to the right answer. There is no writing equivalent of plugging the variables into a formula; you have to come up with your own formula.

In 2001, our family was involved in an accident in which the Ford Explorer I was driving slid onto the median of Interstate 80 and rolled over. My daughter lost a finger in the accident; the rest of us were spared serious injury, though we could have been killed. At the time, the Ford Explorer had been involved in a number of such rollover accidents. Ford was denying that there were any design flaws with the Explorer; the company blamed the rollover accidents on defective tires. Based on my experience in the crash—particularly how quickly the vehicle had rolled when we slid into ice on the highway median—I was convinced that the top-heavy design of the Ford Explorer was the problem, not the tires. I wanted to write an op-ed to that effect. The thesis was clear in my mind: *The Ford Explorer is a dangerous vehicle.*

My audience was clear, too. I was pitching the piece as an op-ed for the *New York Times,* which meant that it would reach informed lay readers. I wanted opinion leaders to read my piece over their morning coffee and be moved by it. I was hoping to be one more voice in a chorus of crusaders seeking to hold Ford accountable for a dangerous vehicle. But what structure should the essay take so that I could translate our experience into a piece that would resonate with strangers?

The scariest thing about the accident was how quickly it happened. One minute we were driving on Interstate 80 listening to *The Hunt for Red October.* Seconds later, we were upside down on the shoulder of the highway hanging from our seatbelts and car seats. The speed with which everything happened during the accident became my narrative tool—*the things I learned quickly.* We were transformed in that moment from people who had read about the Explorer controversy into victims of it. I used the suddenness of the accident and the scariness of the aftermath as the narrative spine for supporting my thesis.

Here is an excerpt from that piece:

Our Ford Explorer felt a lot less practical as we lay smashed upside down in it on Interstate 80 at 4:00 a.m. last Wednesday. My wife was trapped in the passenger seat. Our two daughters hung from their car seats screaming. The dog was silent.[*]

I learned a lot of things very quickly. Each of our girls screams in a slightly different way, and now I know that it is a good thing to hear both screams coming from inside a crushed vehicle—because it means that everyone is alive.

I learned that I can unhook a child from a car seat upside down in the dark with hands so cold that they have lost nearly all sensation.

I know that when there is no other way to get a six-month-old out of a crushed vehicle sitting dangerously close to traffic, you will drag her through broken glass.

I learned that strangers will stop in the middle of the night and practice remarkable acts of kindness, including searching through the wreckage for a missing finger.[†]

---

[*] He was unhurt.

[†] Ford eventually admitted culpability for the design of the Ford Explorer. Later models were redesigned to make them less prone to rollovers.

What will be your narrative structure? This is a question you must answer whether you are writing a one-page marketing document or a six-hundred-page book. No amount of beautiful prose will make up for a narrative structure that does not work. That would be like a lawyer who speaks in beautiful sentences without building a coherent case.

Broadly speaking, how are you going to tell your story?

6. Make an outline.

The outline is a blueprint for your document.

An outline formalizes the narrative structure and gets you to a place where you can start writing. This is the detailed plan for bringing your vision to fruition. Let's return to the architectural example. Suppose your town has decided that you need a new community center with a gymnasium, a childcare center, and several public meeting spaces. *That's your thesis.*

Next, you figure out what this building is going to look like. In public policy circles, this is literally called a "visioning process." The planning committee decides that the building must be environmentally friendly and cannot cost more than $20 million. The town offers a building site: a two-acre lot that can comfortably accommodate a three-story building. The childcare center needs a separate entrance. The gymnasium must also function as a dance studio. There must be two public meeting rooms and office space for the staff. That's the vision for what this community center should look like: *the narrative structure.*

But you are still not ready to pour cement or pound nails. The next step is to hire an architect to draw up blueprints. These detailed plans describe where the elevators will go, how wide the doorways will be, what materials will be used on the exterior, and all the other important details that make it possible to construct a building. *Your outline is the writing equivalent of a blueprint.*

An outline is the backbone of your document. It should describe all the important ideas in the order you plan to cover them. You can use roman numerals for your outline, as you may have been taught in middle school, or you can use bullet points or numbers. The organization is what matters, not the symbols you use to do it. If I were writing an outline for a letter of recommendation for a student, I might begin with the key points I want to cover:

1. My general positive impression of the student
2. Her performance in Public Policy 40
3. Description of the student's independent study on obesity
4. Personality traits that will enable her to thrive in a PhD program

My letter needs to cover these things. It is the order in which I plan to cover them. But there is still room to add detail to my outline. I can add subpoints to further flesh out what I plan to write:

1. My general positive impression of the student
2. Her performance in Public Policy 40
   a. Earned an A– (median was a B+)
   b. Excellent research paper on Medicare drug pricing
3. Description of the student's independent study on obesity
   a. Examined the relationship between high-fructose corn syrup and obesity
   b. Worked with advisors in three different academic departments: biology, sociology, and public policy
   c. Project clearly demonstrates the capacity to do a doctoral dissertation
4. Personality traits that will enable her to thrive in a PhD program
   a. Intellectually curious
   b. Hard-working
   c. Eager to do interdisciplinary work that will have social impact
   d. One of the best students I have worked with in the last five years

This kind of outline requires thought, but not brilliant writing. Most of the points are not complete sentences. Still, you should notice two things. First, the outline has lots of important information. In fact, if I were to send the outline to the graduate program requesting a letter of recommendation, they would learn much of what they need to know just by looking at my numbers and letters. Second, now that I have an outline, my letter is going to be easy to write.

The key to not getting lost in a writing project is doing an outline *before* you begin typing sentences and paragraphs. Students sometimes show up in my office when a writing project isn't going well. They show me pages of written material and folders of information. I often give them one piece of blank paper and say: "Write an outline of what you are trying to do." Similarly, when students begin an independent study, a project that will culminate with a sixty- or eighty-page research paper, my first requirement is that students submit a detailed outline, usually after they have done three or four weeks of research. Most of the students who engage in this process are surprised by how easy it is to write a first draft.

As a correspondent for *The Economist*, I typically spent a week or more gathering information on a story, such as identity theft or compulsive gambling or methamphetamine use. By the time I was done with my reporting, I would have a file an inch thick with reports, interviews, press releases, academic papers. My allotted word count was usually about nine hundred words. If I were to begin typing without a plan, my story would be a string of quotes, vignettes, and anecdotes that would exceed the word count without conveying the essence of what I was trying to report.

As the deadline approached, I wrestled with the complexity of the story. How was I going to organize all this information—the myriad facts, opinions, interesting science, clever quotes? The solution was an outline, often on a piece of scrap paper. To someone looking over my shoulder, the outline would appear remarkably crude, just a bunch of phrases running down the page. But once I settled on a structure that worked, the piece felt nearly done.

- Introduction: Something clever later
- Thesis: Meth is a big problem in America's rural areas, as are other kinds of substance abuse, even though drug use in urban areas gets more attention
- Describe what meth is
- Explain who uses it and why: "blue collar drug of choice"
  - Athletes
  - Long-haul truckers, shift workers, etc.
- Why meth is bad
  - Changes brain chemistry, which is what makes it so addictive
  - Causes aggression
- Larger point and surprise: drug use among young people in rural areas is more common than in urban areas, despite stereotypes
  - Meth can be made from stuff bought at the pharmacy
  - Califano quote about drugs not being just an urban problem
- Describe bad health outcomes
  - With meth use
  - Other drug and alcohol harms also bad in rural areas
  - Needle use causes high rates of HIV/AIDS
- Explain what policymakers are trying to do about it (Clinton admin stuff)
- Clever concluding sentence

Now I had a plan for telling my story. Yes, there were only about a hundred words and very few complete sentences, but that outline was the blueprint for my piece. The thesis was clear. I had identified every key point I wanted to make. I knew the order in which I would present those ideas and where I would insert various facts and quotes. At that point, I just had to turn the ideas into sentences and paragraphs, almost like a paint-by-number kit.

Sometimes an outline will make clear that your narrative structure does not work. Or it may reveal redundancies: you realize that point six is just a restatement of point two. Fixing these problems in the outline stage is much easier than trying to rescue an eleven-page paper—just as it's easier to revise blueprints than it is to have your contractor knock down the building and start over. Once you are comfortable with the outline, good writing means executing against the plan. In fact, with a good outline, you don't even have to start writing at the beginning. If you know what each piece looks like and where it goes, you can work on them independently and then stick them together later, like Legos. In fact, this is a nice indicator of whether you are ready to begin writing: *Am I sufficiently comfortable with my outline that I could begin writing anywhere in the document and still know how it will turn out?*

Too many writers begin by typing, which is not writing. If you begin a complaint letter to the condo board by typing the first things that come to mind, you are doing the equivalent of building a skyscraper without architectural drawings. Maybe you will get lucky. The thoughts may flow coherently.

But it is far more likely that you'll end up with a garbled mess. (Putting your complaints in ALL CAPITALS will not fix the problem.) Computers and other electronic devices have contributed to this problem by making it too easy to bang away at the keyboard without a clear idea of what you are trying to accomplish. These kinds of technology don't make it easier to write; *they make it easier to type.*

Yes, you can add, delete, or cut and paste later; but that is more of a trap than an aid. I suspect many of my students would write better papers if I made them use a manual typewriter. It forces better organization. Obviously, a manual typewriter is impractical for most writing, but you can still use the organizational tools that were essential when it was more costly to fix errors after they were on the page. Write out your thesis. Outline the ideas and points that support the thesis. Add the facts, quotations, and other supporting material where they fit best. Toss out the things that don't fit. Get the blueprint right so that you won't have to move walls later.

If you set out on a road trip without looking at a map, you will soon be lost. *But you are not lost because you are a bad driver.* You are lost because you did not plan your journey before you left the driveway. Similarly, if you find that your prose is muddled and meandering halfway through a paper, it does not mean you are a bad writer. More likely, you have organized your writing poorly. An outline will fix that, just like a good map.

7. Now write complete sentences.

Once you have a clear thesis and a good
outline, it is time to begin writing.

For people who are not comfortable writing, this is the excruciating part: *the blank page*. There is a temptation to do laundry or check email instead. If you are staring at the screen or page without having done any organizational prep work, then it should feel excruciating—*because you are not ready*. It is the writing equivalent of standing at the starting line of a marathon without having trained. You look at the svelte athletes in spandex confidently limbering up and think, "This is not going to go well for me." *And it won't.*

Obviously if you have been training for nine months, the race will go better. That is how you should feel when you begin writing. The prep work you have done to this point—formulating a thesis, developing a narrative structure, and writing an outline—is your training! The blank page is less intimidating when you know what needs to be written in what order. Take the ideas from your outline and turn them into complete sentences.

It is not excruciatingly hard to convert a clear thought into a complete sentence. That is why I always felt so relieved when I had an outline for the stories I was writing for *The Economist*. Let's return to the methamphetamine piece. The thesis was: *Meth is a big problem in America's rural areas, as are other kinds of substance abuse, even though drug use in urban areas gets more attention.* That's a pretty good starting point. One does not have to be Charles Dickens to improve it slightly: *Teenagers in rural areas of the United States are more likely to use methamphetamine and other illegal drugs than their urban peers, despite common stereotypes.*

The same is true with other points on the outline, such as why meth is common in rural areas: *All the ingredients necessary to "cook" the stuff, such as cold medicine, drain cleaner, and lithium batteries, can be found at the local supermarket.* Boom: another sentence.

Just keep going. If you string enough sentences together in the order in which you have arranged them, you will soon have a rough draft. *These do not have to be beautiful sentences.* If you produce a sentence that is consistent with your thesis, conforms to your outline, and has a subject and a verb, then you are on your way. If you type two such sentences, you have written twice as much. Just keep putting one ugly sentence after the other. There will be plenty of time to make them beautiful. (After all, we are only on #7.) To paraphrase the Chinese proverb (and common bumper sticker), a document of a thousand words begins with one sentence supporting your thesis.

Let's do another example. Imagine that your boss has proposed eliminating the office lunch break to promote productivity. Her email has just gone out: *All employees will now be expected to eat at their desks.* You have decided to compose a response arguing that this is a terrible idea. You have jotted down a short outline on the back of a parking ticket, and it looks like this:

Thesis: Eliminating the lunch break is a horrible idea because it will make people angry and unproductive.

1. No one likes to be micromanaged.
2. People need the lunch hour to do other tasks.
3. Having a little break at lunch makes people more productive in the afternoon.
4. If just one person quits, any productivity gains will be more than erased by that loss since it is hard to find qualified workers.

Writing those sentences was easy because it was just jotting down thoughts. But now that those thoughts are organized on the back of the parking ticket, you have a foundation for a cogent email response. Don't overthink it. Just write sentences that are consistent with the ideas you are trying to express.

Start at the beginning with an introduction that encapsulates your thesis:

Dear Cruella,

I am writing to express my belief that the new lunch policy requiring workers to eat at their desks is not something I support. It will make people angry because they don't like being told what to do and it might actually make people less productive in the long run.

Yuck. This is not Proust. "I'm writing to express my belief" . . . Well, of course you are. You are not writing to express someone else's beliefs, are you? The second sentence uses "it" twice. But you know what? The structure works and the sentences get your point across. You can buff and polish the prose in the second draft.

Now do the same thing for the next paragraph.

Our workers take pride in what they do and do not like to be told how to do it. This new lunch policy will be interpreted as unnecessary micromanagement.

That's not so bad. One could quibble over whether "unnecessary micromanagement" is redundant. Do you know when you are going to worry about that? *Later.* For now, you've got two functional paragraphs. You cannot make a beautiful marble statue without first carving something rough and ugly. Perfect is the enemy of good—in life, but especially with first drafts. For that matter, do not even aim for good. Let's aim for *not awful.* (Yes, the phrase "not awful" might be construed as a double negative, which is a grammar faux pas. See #33: "Once you know the rules, you can consider disregarding them.")

How do you overcome that daunting blank page? Not by watching Netflix, checking your phone, or taking a run. You do it by turning the ideas in your outline into complete sentences. Also, don't forget to pay the parking ticket once you are done with the outline.

8. Use paragraphs as the building blocks of your document.

Each important idea deserves its own paragraph.

Paragraphs do two things, one substantive and the other aesthetic. Substantively, paragraphs lead the reader through the important points you are trying to make. The paragraphs in your rough draft should coincide with the points on your outline. For example, if you are writing a newsletter article describing the annual student athlete awards, your outline might look something like this:

- Description of the criteria for the Student Athlete of the Year awards
  - Excellent grades over four years
  - Contributions to the community
- Kati Madden
  - Varsity swimming
  - 3.89 GPA
  - Advocate for mental health awareness
- Sam Pych
  - Soccer captain
  - Leading scorer, three years
  - Academic All Conference
  - Special Olympics volunteer
- Recognition for winners
  - Plaque in the Student Activities hallway
  - $50 Target gift card

There are four logical paragraphs: a description of the award; a description of the women's winner; a description of the men's winner; and a final paragraph describing how the winners will be recognized. The paragraphs lead the reader through each important idea. If all of that information were crammed into one dense paragraph, the reader would find it much harder to absorb the information. In his memo on better memo-writing, Churchill admonished his war cabinet, "The aim should be Reports which set out the main points in a series of short, crisp paragraphs."

Meanwhile, paragraphs help aesthetically because they break up long blocks of text. When I am grading student papers, I sometimes skip those with a first page that has one long, single-spaced paragraph. That dense wall of text signals to me that I am going to have to work harder to read the essay. Even before I have read a single word, the formatting exhausts me because it suggests that the writer has not given any thought to making the document reader-friendly.

Imagine yourself in a restaurant where you order a chocolate dessert. When the waiter brings the dessert from the kitchen, it is an ugly dense blob on the plate. Your first impression is that it looks uncomfortably similar to something that a dog might leave behind on a patch of grass. "It's delicious," the waiter insists. And maybe it is. *But it certainly doesn't look delicious.* The uninviting appearance of the dish makes you less eager to dig in with a spoon. This is why good chefs pay attention to presentation as well as taste. If a dish comes out of the kitchen looking like someone stepped on it with a boot, there is a good chance that the chef has paid little attention to other details, like flavor. The same is true with writing: If you produce a document that looks dense and foreboding, why would the reader expect something well-organized and pleasant to read?

Of course, the aesthetic and the substance are related. Overly long paragraphs are daunting for the reader because they have packed together ideas that deserve their own treatment. There is a relatively simple check: If you have a long paragraph, how related are the ideas at the end of the paragraph to those at the beginning? If your paragraph begins with a sentence describing the rules of rugby and finishes with three sentences on the history of New Zealand's Maori people, you need to separate those distinct ideas. The good news is that there is a simple fix: find the place where you transition from one idea to another—such as the point where you finish describing the female Student Athlete of the Year and introduce the male winner—and insert a paragraph break there.

Writing is a lot easier if you think of any document as an accumulation of well-organized paragraphs. Anyone can write a decent paragraph, especially if the content hews closely to your outline. And if you can write one good paragraph, you can write many good paragraphs. It's the grown-up version of playing with blocks.

9. Get the grammar right.

Grammar is the set of rules that allows us to organize language, like traffic laws for words.

A piece of writing with poor grammar is like a busy intersection without functioning traffic lights: a mess (though perhaps less dangerous). I have taught university students for nearly two decades. I have never read great writing with bad grammar. Not once. True, some brilliant writers bend the rules of grammar, but they invariably understand the rules before choosing to disregard them. For now, grammar is the instruction manual for coherent writing.

A piece of writing that is grammatically correct may not be elegant, but it will be clear and readable. Conversely, even the most brilliant ideas can be obscured or confused by bad grammar. The combination of bad grammar and poor organization is particularly toxic. Those are the student essays that I work hard to understand before eventually giving up and writing across the top of the first page, "Let's talk about this."

This book is not a primer on good grammar. Other books have done that well, notably *The Elements of Style* by Strunk and White. More recently, *Dreyer's English* is an entertaining and comprehensive book on English usage written by Benjamin Dreyer, former copy chief at Random House. *The Economist* has an excellent style guide that focuses on brevity and clarity. (For example, a "wilderness area" is redundant; just call it wilderness.) You will have to learn your grammar elsewhere. However, I will highlight some of the most common grammatical errors that turn sensible ideas into a muddle on the page.

Subject-verb agreement: When the subject and verb of a sentence do not match, the effect is jarring. This happens most frequently when a writer does not understand the true subject of the sentence. Consider this painful example: *One of the tanks were broke*n. Did you instinctively go back and read that sentence a second time? Yes, "tanks" is plural, but the subject of the sentence is "one" of those tanks. One is singular. The sentence should be: *One of the tanks was broken*.

In general, if someone has to read your sentence twice, it is a lousy sentence.

Parallel structure in a series: When a sentence involves multiple items in a series, they must match: *My wife is smart, generous, and kind.* The three descriptors are all adjectives. *I plan to go shopping, to make dinner, and to clean up the dishes.* Those three activities are all verbs in their infinitive form. I could write a similar sentence: *I plan to help out by shopping, making dinner, and cleaning up the dishes.* Those are all verbs in the gerund form. Is it essential that you know what a gerund is? No. But you must recognize that you can't write this sentence: *I plan to go shopping, to make dinner, and cleaning up the dishes.*

Run-on sentences: Grammar is like computer code; each sentence offers a discrete action. Punctuation and other tools, such as conjunctions, are the signals that allow our brains to interpret the code. *I climbed out of bed, took a shower, and recy-*

cled the whisky bottles. That is one sentence with three actions. The commas and the use of "and" in the series make the actions clear.

Now consider the following sentence, which is so painful that I'm having trouble writing it (and grammar check is not happy with me either): *Saheer came to the office even though I had no idea he was coming I fired him Ron didn't know either and agreed with me.* What a mess. My brain is screaming, *No!* Obviously, I have deliberately engineered such a mess, but the problem with the sentence is figuring out what happened to whom. How would you go about making sense of it? By dividing the sentence up into its different actions. That is what good grammar should have done in the first place. *Saheer came to the office. I had no idea he was coming. I fired him. Ron also did not know Saheer was coming and agreed with my decision to fire him.*

Clear antecedents: Pronouns—he, she, it, they, and so on—are handy tools for referring back to people and things you have already identified. However, pronouns only work if it is clear who or what they are referring to. Imagine that you have stumbled onto a ticking bomb in a crowded stadium. You have heroically volunteered to defuse it. The timer on the bomb indicates that there are twenty seconds until detonation. You are on the phone with the head of the bomb squad, who instructs you: *There is a plastic cap, an orange wire, and a small wad of plastic explosive. You have five seconds to pull it out.* I have never been in such a situation, but my sense is that you would scream into the phone, *"What is 'it'?" You listed*

three things and then used 'it' without telling me which one it is!"
This is an example of unclear antecedent; the reader does not
know what "it" refers to.

Let's return to our mess in the office involving Ron and
Saheer: *Saheer came to the office. I had no idea he was coming,
nor did Ron, who got very angry and started yelling. I fired him.*
Whom did I fire, Ron or Saheer? Reading a sentence should
not feel like detective work. In the case of an unclear antecedent, there is a simple fix: use the noun to which it refers
instead. *I fired Saheer.*

Now I turn to the most painful part of this section: real
examples from papers that students have submitted to me:

*The IPCC report, as well as other organizations, find human
carbon emissions to be one of the largest contributors to climate
change.* The problem with this sentence is that the IPCC
report is not an organization; it's a report. As a result, the
clause "as well as other organizations" does not make sense.
There is a subject-verb agreement problem, too. The subject
of this sentence is "report," which is singular. The verb ought
to be "finds." And finally, if we are being persnickety, "the
report" did not find carbon emissions to be contributors to climate change; the authors of the report did.

This idea could be more clearly expressed the following
way: *The authors of the IPCC report concluded that human carbon emissions are one of the largest contributors to climate change.
Other organizations have come to the same conclusion.* Two clear
sentences are better than a single muddled one.

Here is another: *The time to begin acting on climate change is long overdue, and it needs to be addressed directly at the source.* The problem here is that "it" has an ambiguous antecedent. The student intended to say that climate change should be addressed directly at the source (e.g., power plants). Instead, the subject of the first clause is "time," so the second clause suggests that what needs to be addressed at the source is "the time to begin acting on climate change"—which makes no sense at all. Again, this important idea could be expressed more clearly: *Climate change needs to be addressed directly at the source, and the time for doing that is long overdue.*

One more: *The recent Stanford study indicates that Chicago's students grow faster than ninety-six percent of the school districts in the country.* This sentence raises the intriguing question of how a student—in Chicago or anywhere else—can grow faster than a school district. The writer was trying to express the fact that students in Chicago demonstrate more learning growth than students do in 96 percent of the country's other school districts.

Okay, the last one: *Despite being largely regulated by the states, there is no historical evidence that federal intervention can have a strong effect on vaccination.* What is regulated by the states? Historical evidence? Not that I'm aware. I don't think any level of government regulates historical evidence. The student is trying to say that vaccination is largely regulated by the states. As a result, federal intervention would not have much impact on vaccination rates. Here are three sentences that make that point more clearly: *The states are responsible for vaccination laws. This means that federal intervention is likely to have little impact on vaccination rates. This is what historical evidence suggests.*

Grammar provides the rules that allow our brain to absorb the written and spoken word. Clear writing requires proper grammar. Long sentences are not inherently improper. Some are brilliant. But as a sentence gets more complex, more can go wrong. When in doubt, stick with short, clear sentences, especially in the first draft. Similarly, if you are having trouble making a sentence clear, break it up. Short sentences may not have the poetic flow of James Joyce, but you are probably not the writer that James Joyce was. And, for the record, most people have a really hard time reading James Joyce. There is a good chance he would be fired from any modern job that requires clear, cogent writing.

Grammar plays another role: it sends a signal to others about your capabilities and professionalism. Would you contribute a million dollars to a nonprofit if the person who comes to your office to make the pitch has a large ketchup stain on his shirt? It (the ketchup stain) suggests incompetence. Bad grammar is the written equivalent of that ketchup stain. A school principal who sends out an email to parents that confuses "their" for "they're" is not sending a great signal about the quality of education in the building. Most word-processing programs have some kind of grammar check. These programs are not perfect, but they can be helpful. At a minimum, if the software flags a phrase or sentence, you should understand why it is being flagged.

Using good grammar is like having the proper equipment

for a sporting competition. Buying an excellent tennis rac-
quet will not ensure that you win the match. But if you walk
onto the court carrying a baseball bat, you are certain to lose
while signaling to everyone watching that you have no idea
what you are doing.

10. Aspire to be clear; avoid inappropriate jargon.

Good writers and speakers communicate
in ways that make them understood.

Every once in a while, I will hear someone offer a variation on
the following statement after they read a document or listen
to a talk by a distinguished person: "I'm not smart enough
to understand that." Nonsense. The reality is that the writer
or speaker was not talented enough to communicate his or
her ideas effectively. That is not a badge of intelligence; it is
a mark of laziness, arrogance, or both. I studied economics
at the University of Chicago. Does that mean I should stand
up at a Rotary Club meeting and say the following: *I support a
carbon tax because the price elasticity of demand of carbon-based
fuels is such that a Pigouvian tax would induce consumers to
internalize the externality associated with carbon emissions.* No.
That sentence is fine for the *American Economic Review*; it is
ridiculous for a lay audience.

All that jargon does not make me a dazzling speaker; it
makes me a pompous jackass who was too lazy to think about
how I could communicate those important ideas to the intel-

ligent people in Rotary who don't happen to have advanced degrees in economics. Who goes out of his way to make people feel ignorant or uninformed? More important, I should not expect anyone in the audience to be persuaded that a carbon tax is good policy, which is presumably the purpose of my talk. (See #1: "Why are you writing this?")

The irony is that the economic jargon can be translated easily into language more appropriate for the Rotary Club: *I support a tax on carbon emissions from fuels like coal and oil because it would be a powerful tool for slowing climate change. Part of the problem with carbon-based fuels is that when we use them, we impose a cost on the rest of society in the form of pollution that we don't have to pay for ourselves. When I get in my car, I pay for the gas and the insurance, but not the carbon emissions that affect the rest of the planet. A carbon tax is essentially a tax on pollution. If we make pollution more expensive, people will do less of it. That's just basic economics.*

That phrasing is longer than the jargon-laced language that I might use with economists. The purpose of technical language, including acronyms, is to express complex ideas succinctly to others who share the same background or expertise. When one soldier asks another about an MRE, they both know that means a Meal, Ready to Eat. There is an efficiency to these kinds of abbreviations. But there is nothing efficient about using technical terms with a nontechnical audience. Does it make you a genius to speak Spanish to an audience that doesn't speak Spanish?

Jargon can disguise sloppy thinking, like the Wizard of Oz hiding behind his curtain. *Trust me because I'm using big words that you can't understand.* When I was teaching graduate students in public policy, I assigned a project in which groups of students proposed a major policy change, such as legalizing marijuana or expanding early childhood education. Each group wrote a long memo with analysis and data supporting their plan. I graded these memos, which meant that students could use whatever technical language best made their case. However, each group also had to write a short opinion piece promoting their plan; this piece had to be suitable for publication in a local newspaper or online. (Most news outlets have a section where outsiders are invited to share their views; in a traditional newspaper, these pieces are called "op-eds" because they are published opposite the editorial page.) The student op-eds had to be short (no more than eight hundred words), and they had to be persuasive for normal newspaper readers.

Here is the twist: I did not grade the op-eds. Instead, I gave them to my wife Leah, who is a quick study but not a public policy expert. If she finished an op-ed and said, "This is a great idea," the group got a good grade on that part of the project. If she finished and said, "I don't understand how this would work," or "What does this mean?" or anything else suggesting the piece was unclear, the group got a lower grade. It was a simple way to assess whether the students could write effectively for a lay audience—and less work for me, too.

Clarity is the foundation of effective communication. If your readers or listeners do not grasp the full and accurate meaning of what you are trying to say, nothing else can make up for that—not alliteration, not iambic pentameter, not words like "exonumia." (And no, I'm not going to tell you what exonumia means because it shouldn't have been in that sentence.) Imagine you have planned an elaborate birthday party for yourself. There will be a live band, catered food, and ice sculptures. Let's watch that party unravel because of your unclear communication.

- The ice sculptures melted a week ago because you told the sculptor to deliver them "next Tuesday." This was a Sunday, and the sculptor assumed that you wanted the ice sculptures delivered in two days. However, since Sunday is the first day of the week, you actually meant Tuesday of the following week (nine days later). If you had said, "Tuesday the 14th," the ice sculptures would not have melted in your garden before the party.

- The guests arrived four hours before the band did. Why? Because you told the band and the invitees that the party would begin "at the end of the day." Your friends and coworkers arrived at five o'clock—the end of the workday. The band assumed that you meant sundown, which was at nine o'clock—about the time that most of the guests were leaving.

- Some guests left much earlier—when they were rushed to the hospital in anaphylactic shock after eating the caterer's peanut butter surprise. Yes, you had informed the caterer that several guests were allergic to legumes. Because you are super smart, you know that peanuts are not technically nuts; they are legumes. How exciting it will be to win trivia night at the local coffee house with that morsel of knowledge! The caterer, however, has never heard of legumes. Therefore, he assumed that the peanut butter surprise appetizers would be a crowd pleaser—and they were, until the paramedics were called to deal with the guests struggling to breathe. (Thankfully, the person who called 911 gave clear directions. The paramedics arrived in time to administer a shot of epinephrine—the contents of an epi pen—and save the guests in anaphylactic shock.)

Clarity is the foundation of effective writing and speaking. If a sentence is long and convoluted, break it into shorter sentences. If there is a word or concept that people may not understand, define that term, or, better yet, use a more widely understood substitute. If an example will clarify an idea or concept, then use an example (like the birthday party gone out of control because of a lack of clarity). If your intended audience does not understand what you are trying to tell them, it is your fault, not theirs.

The Economist is considered to be a particularly clever and well-written publication. Here is an excerpt from the *The Economist Style Guide*: "The first requirement of *The Economist* is that it should be readily understandable. Clarity of writing usually follows clarity of thought. So think what you want to say, then say it as simply as possible."[5]

The most impressive experts are not those who write and speak in ways that confound their audience. Rather, they are people who can communicate complex ideas in ways that are easily grasped by all.

11. Always be framing.

Framing is the use of strategic language
to provoke an emotional response.

All words have meaning. Some words also prompt an emotional response. Framing is the strategic use of language to make an idea attractive on a visceral level (or to repel us emotionally from an opposing idea). Regular language speaks to our brain; framing speaks to our gut. The goal is to choose words and phrases that pack an emotional punch.

Consider the language often used around the issue of abortion, which is a contentious political issue in America. The supporters and opponents of abortion rights do not typically describe themselves as "pro-abortion" or "anti-abortion."

Rather, those who support legal access to abortion tend to describe themselves as "pro-choice." This framing focuses one's attention on *a woman's right to choose.*

Opponents of legalized abortion describe themselves as "pro-life." They are *protecting the life of an unborn child.*

Like a picture frame, strategic language affects how we see an issue by directing focus to the most emotionally resonant aspect of a position: "choice" and "life."

Strategic language figures prominently in the immigration debate as well. What do we call people who enter the United States illegally? Well, that depends on how we want to frame the phenomenon. Proponents of more relaxed immigration laws tend to refer to this population as *undocumented workers.* "Work" and "workers" are powerfully positive words in America; "undocumented" suggests one has neglected to fill out tedious paperwork. Taken together, the phrase *undocumented worker* suggests that someone forgot to fill out the right form in an effort to join the American workforce and make our country stronger.

Opponents of immigration sometimes refer to persons who enter the country without authorization as *illegal aliens*. That phrase packs an emotional punch. "Illegal" draws attention to the fact that these people have broken the law. "Alien" is a term that reinforces their otherness, especially since "aliens" in pop culture tend to be invaders from outer space. By this framing, *illegal aliens* are strange people with potentially hostile intent who have entered the country by breaking the law.

Framing can take on a surreal aspect when different factions refuse to use the same language in the course of their disagreement. If you were involved in discussions between the Israelis and the Palestinians, for example, you might find yourself discussing the geographic area controlled by Israel between the Jordan River and the Jordanian border. How you chose to refer to this roughly two-thousand-square-mile area would say a lot about your politics. To many outsiders, including US journalists and diplomats, this area is known as the West Bank. That is a literal description, as the land is located on the west bank of the Jordan River.

For many Palestinians, this is the land where they would like to see a future Palestinian state; they refer to it as Palestine or Occupied Palestine. Israeli government officials might refer to that area as Judea and Samaria; these are Biblical references to that geographic place that reinforce the idea that the land was part of the ancient Kingdom of Israel.

This section is not meant to be a primer on Middle East politics. Rather, it is meant to show how the strategic use of language can affect how ideas are interpreted—*literally, how the brain processes them*. To illustrate the power of framing, let me take you back to 2002 when one of my responsibilities for *The Economist* was analyzing the annual FBI violent-crime data and writing a short story on any key trends. When I received the data, I was surprised to see that there had been a large jump in homicides in the previous year. Violent crime had been trending down for more than a decade. Why had I not heard anything about a spike in homicides? Were the data wrong? Or was there some significant uptick in murders that had gone unreported?

Neither. The FBI crime statistics for 2001 (the previous year) included the 3,047 people murdered on September 11. The definition of homicide is the killing of one human by another. By that definition, the deaths on 9/11 belonged in the homicide statistics. In my brain, that is not where I had filed them—because "terrorism" was a different mental bucket than "homicide." The words affected how I processed reality.

Psychologists have found that much of our thinking is done at an emotional or intuitive level. We think we are making an intellectual decision; in fact, we are often doing what our "gut" tells us to do. Jonathan Haidt, a professor at NYU and the author of *The Righteous Mind*, has come up with the metaphor of an elephant and a rider. He explains, "The rider is our conscious reasoning—the stream of words and images of which we are fully aware. The elephant is the other 99 percent of mental processes—the ones that occur outside of awareness but actually govern most of our behavior."[6] The rider thinks he is in control, but the elephant's decisions are the ones that matter. If you want to change people's minds, Haidt insists, you need to speak to their elephants. That is what framing does.

There are experts, particularly in politics, who use polling and focus groups to determine what words will sell an issue or position best. For example, Republican pollster Frank Luntz is famous for his brilliant use of framing. He is the one who rebranded the "estate tax" as the "death tax." A *Frontline* special on Luntz's work noted, "When it was called the estate tax, most people supported it. But Luntz managed to turn public opinion against it simply by giving it an emotionally loaded new name."[7]

In the same program, political activist Rob Stein, who does not share Luntz's political views, laments, "Frank Luntz doesn't do issues. He does language around issues. He figures out what words will best sell an issue—and he polls them, and he tests them, and he focus-groups them—and he comes up, issue by issue, with how to talk about it and how not to talk about it."

All of this may feel manipulative—*because it is*. When you are writing, you get to choose the language. Your language should reflect what you are trying to accomplish. In the David

Mamet play *Glengarry Glen Ross* (later adapted into a film), a group of salespeople are struggling to sell real estate. Their boss admonishes them: "Always be closing." What he means is that from the moment a conversation begins with a client, a good salesperson will be focused on closing the deal. When writing, always be framing. Use strategic language, particularly in your introduction and conclusion, to frame your position. If you don't frame your position, someone else will—and it may not be to your liking.

12. Give credit where credit is due.

*Identify the source for any thought, idea, photo,
graph, or fact that was generated by someone else.*

Don't steal. This is a widely accepted social and legal norm. You should not walk out of a convenience store with your pockets full of merchandise that you did not pay for. You should not take jewelry from the homes of your friends (or, for that matter, from people who are not your friends). And you should not steal the ideas of others. True, stealing ideas will probably not land you in prison, but it might get you fired or thrown out of school. I teach at Dartmouth College, where appropriating someone else's work will get you what students refer to as "a Parkhurst vacation." Parkhurst is the building for administrative offices; the vacation is an involuntary suspension.

But here is the crazy thing about great quotations and ideas: *You should never have to steal them, because you can bor-*

row whatever you want. All you have to do is give credit to the owner. It is like being able to borrow the most beautiful clothes and jewelry in the world, as long as you make clear that they belong to someone else. "Do you like this forty-five-carat diamond? It's called the Hope Diamond. The Smithsonian lets me use it when I go out to formal events." *Just give credit to the owner and it's yours to wear!*

English teachers often obsess over the format of citations: MLA or Chicago style or some other set of rules about where the commas and periods go. As you might infer from the tone of the previous sentence, I have no preference about the format of citations, as long as they do two things. First, the citation should give appropriate credit to the source of the original idea or material. *I'm glad you like my diamond. It belongs to the Smithsonian Museum.*

Second, the citation should allow the reader to find a source that you have referred to. In this book, I refer several times to the memo Winston Churchill sent to his war cabinet urging them to write better memos. I first learned about this memo in Erik Larson's excellent book on Churchill's leadership during the Blitz on London, *The Splendid and the Vile.* In the book, Larson alluded to one passage from this Churchill memo. I wanted to read the whole thing. I looked up the citation at the end of Larson's book. That led me to a volume of Churchill's war papers at the Dartmouth College library. On page 636, I found Churchill's full memo admonishing his cabinet to write better.

When should you use a citation? According to *The Chi-*

cago Manual of Style, "Ethics, copyright laws, and courtesy to readers require authors to identify the sources of direct quotations and of any facts or opinions not generally known or easily checked."[8] You do not need to footnote information that is considered common knowledge, such as the fact that the world is round, or that Meryl Streep is an actress.

At the risk of being too self-congratulatory, let me review what I accomplished in that paragraph. *I described when to use a citation by using a citation.* The beauty of quoting *The Chicago Manual of Style* is that I did not have to spend a lot of time coming up with language of my own to describe when content in your writing needs to be documented. Instead, I borrowed the excellent work of someone else and gave them credit for it. It is the writing equivalent of borrowing the Hope Diamond. Or, to make the same point differently, why would I plagiarize someone's work when I can use it so easily by inserting a note?

With some kinds of writing, offering a source provides another advantage: it bestows credibility on your argument. For this reason, it can make sense to identify your source in the body of the document rather than in a footnote or endnote. Often my students will write something like: *An economist concluded in a recent report that a carbon tax is the most cost-effective way to manage climate change.* The economist and the study are properly cited at the bottom of the page or the end of the memo, which is fine from a plagiarism standpoint. Credit has been given where credit is due. But there are a lot of "economists" in the world producing lots of "reports." Some of those economists live in their parents' basements and send out tweets to eleven followers. Others work at world-class universities, publish in peer-reviewed journals, and have won the Nobel Prize.

If the economist is one of the latter rather than the former, you should advertise that in the body of the memo: "*A University of Chicago economist* noted in a recent report *published by the Brookings Institution . . .* " These details convey information. The fact that the economist works at the University of Chicago means that he or she is at a top university famous for its economics department. The Brookings Institution is a prominent Washington think tank. By including this information in the body of the memo, you have told the reader that this is a report produced by a credible economist and published by a respected institution. Yes, the reader could have found all that in a footnote, but if this is something that lends credibility to your case, why bury it in the small print?

Give credit to others. It is the right thing to do, and it makes you look smarter, too. If you steal a clever phrase from Martin Luther King Jr. and use it in your work, you are a plagiarizer. If you use the same passage with attribution, you are thoughtful and well-read.

13. When working in a group, create a process that shares the workload and gathers input from all participants while still producing a coherent document.

Something written by a group should not
read like it was written by a group.

Yes, many hands make for light work. When it comes to writing, many hands also make for squabbling, free-riding, and insipid prose. When someone says, "This reads like it was written by committee," that is not usually high praise. Anything with multiple authors is at risk of lacking focus. At worst, the document can become redundant or internally inconsistent. The importance of narrative structure—and the crucial point that any story can be told many ways—was covered earlier (#5). In a group of seven people, there might be seven reasonable suggestions for a narrative structure. To be coherent, your document can only have one. Similarly, every writer has his or her own "voice," which is the style and tone they write with. When multiple writers collaborate, these voices may collide, which is why artists rarely collaborate on a single piece of work. The vision is lost; the voice is muddled. Imagine three people trying to do one watercolor painting at the same time.

When I was in graduate school, all the students in my cohort, roughly sixty students, were given the task of working together to write a policy memo on how America could ameliorate its growing homelessness problem. We reckoned that the finished memo would be fifty or sixty pages. There were sixty people contributing to the project, so some quick math revealed that we would each have to write a page or so. How hard could that be? We would cobble those pages together quickly and be done with the project (and maybe homelessness, too).

The early drafts demonstrated that our challenge was not typing sixty pages; it was formulating cogent, consistent recommendations for reducing homelessness and then conveying them in a coherent way. Sixty contributors produced a hodgepodge. Some sections were overly long. Others lacked detail. Many of our proposals were inconsistent or contradictory. For a while, we had trouble getting the fonts to match.

We were eventually able to match the fonts, but that was the only thing about the document that suggested unity of thought. It was as if we had invited sixty people to a construction site and told them to pick up some tools and begin building a house. We had nothing approximating an architectural drawing. In despair, we voted to create an editorial committee to oversee production of the document. Unfortunately, we did not ask any of the people nominated if they wanted to serve on the editorial committee. The group met and immediately voted to disband itself. We began referring to the assignment as "The Hopelessness Project."

Even Martin Luther King Jr. fell victim to writing by committee. Jon Meacham notes in his excellent podcast on historical speeches that King's "I Have a Dream" speech was written the night before by a group of staffers. As King delivered the speech before some two hundred and fifty thousand people, he struggled with some of the clunky language. He reached one particularly awkward committee-generated sentence: "And so today, let us go back to our communities as members of the international association for the advancement of creative dissatisfaction."[9] Dr. King decided to depart from the text and extemporize. Not long after, he heard a woman's voice in the crowd. It was gospel singer Mahalia Jackson, who yelled, "Tell them about the dream, Martin." In that moment, Dr. King adopted the "I have a dream" motif that came to characterize the speech.

In general, you should not toss aside your prepared text—because you are not MLK. But there are two lessons from this historical moment. First, multiple authors can create a mess, even when they are writing for Martin Luther King Jr. And second, "I have a dream . . ." turned out to be a brilliant narrative structure for delivering his civil rights message.

Much of professional life requires collaboration. At its best, collaborative writing, like any group work, incorporates diverse voices, builds consensus, and spreads the workload. At its worst, people begin tossing around words like "hopelessness." To get the best out of group writing, you must design a process that creates a chorus from multiple voices rather than a cacophony. This requires more than a shared document on Google drive. Here are things you can do to facilitate group writing:

Elect an editor or team leader: This person is not more important than the others. He or she is not necessarily a better writer. Rather, this is the person who has responsibility for organizing the work, like the conductor of a symphony. The editor can make assignments, monitor deadlines, read drafts, manage the technology, and do other things that require some centralized coordination. It is reasonable for this person to do less writing in exchange for his or her managerial contributions.

Tackle the free-rider problem: One of the reasons people dislike group work is that there always seems to be one guy who would rather binge-watch Netflix than do his share of the work. The remedy for this problem is context specific, but there must be some mechanism for dealing with it. A good start is agreeing on what is expected of each group member and then enforcing those expectations. "Sheryl, I see that you were supposed to write an introduction and a conclusion and post them to the shared drive by 5:00 this evening. It looks like all you have posted so far is a picture of your cat." Being transparent about what work has been assigned and what work has been completed can be a powerful motivator. If you are in a professional work environment, it is reasonable to share this information with the person in charge, such as the manager of a consulting project or the head of sales.

When I assign a group project, I ask the group to do an evaluation of each member after the project is completed. Specifically, I require that each person submit an anonymous evaluation of the contribution of every group member, including themselves, on a scale of 1 (no meaningful participation) to 5 (a great team member). *This is not a ranking.* What I like to see is all 5s—everyone in the group was pleased with the effort of everyone else. This is a relatively simple way to monitor the shirkers. There is no surefire fix for free riders, but any system that makes expectations clear and holds participants accountable will help.

Create a process for making revisions: The only thing worse than five people writing at once is five people editing a document at the same time. Yes, technology makes this possible; no, it is not a good idea. One person might be expanding a paragraph only to have another person cut it entirely—and so on. There must be a mechanism for coordinating the group's feedback into a single set of changes. The editor might be tasked with that job. Or you may do a table read, in which the group goes through the document together, gathering input from all participants and agreeing on changes. The important thing is that diverse feedback is melded into a single set of edits.

Decide how you will resolve disputes: People do not always agree. This can be a strength of group projects: dissenting opinions help to overcome groupthink. Or it can be a major problem if dissenting opinions lead to fistfights. At the beginning of the project—before any disputes arise—the group should determine a mechanism for resolving disagreements.

Perhaps the group will vote when there is a disagreement, with the majority getting its way. Or the elected editor may be empowered to resolve disputes. *Just have a process.* When I was a speechwriter for the governor of Maine, I was responsible for writing the State of the State Address. One year, as the speech was refined late at night with input from ambitious members of the administration, I ended up in a screaming match with a member of the cabinet over the definition of "neighbor." I insisted that a neighbor is anyone who lives in the general vicinity of one's home; she argued that a neighbor has to be physically adjacent to one's property. Our dispute resolution method was simple: it was the governor's speech, so he decided. I am proud to say that he agreed with my definition of neighbor. On the other hand, the woman I was arguing with is now a US senator.[*]

Agree on as much as possible before the writing begins: This is a case where "having everyone on the same page" is literally true. At the outset, a group should create a set of informal rules, many of which have already been discussed. The group can also agree on an outline, or some other vision for the project. The rules and the outline function like a contract among the group members: This is what we are going to do, and here is how we are going to do it.

All of this applies to presentations as well. There are few things more awkward than four people at the front of the

[*] Maine senator Susan Collins.

room staring at each other as they try to figure out who will speak next.

GROUP MEMBER #1: Are you going to explain why the Democrats opposed the tax plan?

GROUP MEMBER #2: I thought you were going to do that.

GROUP MEMBER #1: I sent you an email asking you to do it.

GROUP MEMBER #2: You should have texted me.

GROUP MEMBER #3: Maybe we should move on to the revenue data.

GROUP MEMBER #2: Alex was supposed to do that slide, and he's not here.

GROUP MEMBER #3: Why isn't he here?

GROUP MEMBER #1: I'm not sure he knew we were presenting today. He has an away cross-country race.

ME: How about if we reschedule your presentation for next week?

The best group projects are better than what can be produced by one person working alone. The worst group projects cause the participants to scream at each other while crying in their professor's office. (Sadly, this is not a hypothetical example.) A good process makes the former more likely than the latter.

14. The first draft is about getting all the important ideas down with grammatically correct sentences and a structure that works.

The clunky but essential first draft can be edited later into something sharper, tighter, and better.

The first draft is a horrible document to behold. The sentences are inelegant. The content is repetitive. Some of the examples are not right. Parts of the draft need to be shorter; others need to be fleshed out with examples. The first draft is the writing equivalent of how most of us feel when we get out of bed in the morning.

But do you know what else a first draft is? *Done.* Once you have an ugly draft, you can begin to do the things to make it beautiful. The crucial prerequisite for any exquisite piece of writing is the lousy first draft that precedes it—the clunky bloc of marble that can be chiseled into something more elegant and polished.

If your first draft is a frog that will become a prince, there are certain essentials. First, every sentence needs a subject and verb. This may seem like silliness, but much of the early stages of my writing consist of sentence fragments and notes to myself: "insert funny story here" and "economists think this is bad" and "data from Brookings." In the first draft, each of these little fragments gets expanded into a complete sentence. As noted earlier, the ideas in the outline become sentences in the draft; those sentences are organized into complete paragraphs, however clunky they may feel.

Second, the organizational structure must work. Future drafts will only become more beautiful if you are comfortable with the narrative structure. Your editing should focus on making each paragraph better, not moving paragraphs around. To return to our construction metaphor, if you have not put the walls in the right place, beautiful paint and wallpaper will not fix the problem. Make sure the walls are where you want them.

Third, all necessary citations should be in place. This may seem like something that can be done later, but that is how mistakes get made. The esteemed historian Doris Kearns Goodwin was accused of plagiarism because of an error like this. According to the *New York Times,* "Ms. Goodwin said the problem stemmed from taking notes and then writing her manuscript in longhand. She said she confused verbatim notes with her own words."[10] See how I gave the *Times* credit for that explanation? That footnote was in the first draft—because I did not want to forget later that I had quoted the *Times.*

Finally, do not ever put something in a draft that you would be embarrassed to see in the final document—because mistakes happen. If you do not know the name of the director of human resources and plan to insert it later, do not refer to him in your first draft as "the guy with the receding hairline." Do not make jokes about your customers or your professor that you plan to cut after you have chuckled about them with your roommate. Why? Because you might submit the wrong file when you turn in the paper. You might email the wrong draft to the whole company. You might leave a copy on the printer. This first draft does not have to make you proud—but it should not get you fired or expelled.

When I assign writing projects to my students, I generally allow one rewrite; the grade is an average of their first and second papers. Paradoxically, my students like the rewrite option. They are not looking to do extra work, but the rewrite gives them an opportunity to fix things they knew could be better, often because the first draft was finished five minutes before class. If an assignment is due electronically at midnight, the papers come flooding in at 11:57 p.m., 11:59 p.m., 12:00 a.m., 12:03 a.m. It's possible that my students have done multiple drafts before uploading a carefully edited version of their paper minutes before (or after) the deadline, but I doubt it based on my subsequent conversations with them. As students sit in my office reviewing my comments, they say things like, "I knew that section was too long" and "Yeah, that didn't make sense to me either" or "I didn't have time to fix that." Their tone is not defensive; instead, they are modestly excited to have an opportunity to make the paper better.

If your first draft is your last draft, you will never be a great writer, or even a good one. But once you have that first draft, the hard part is over. You have climbed out of bed and are standing in the bathroom. You have not showered or brushed your teeth or had your morning coffee.

Still, you are out of bed. Things will get better from here.

MAKING IT BETTER

15. Write an introduction that grabs the reader and encapsulates the entire document.

Your introduction must do two things:
(1) Convey to readers the big idea of the piece;
and (2) Persuade them to continue reading.

In school, teachers are paid to read what you write, from start to finish. Once you graduate, no one will have that obligation. In life, your writing will only reach people if they choose to read it. And they will only read it if your introduction is sufficiently enticing to urge them on. Readers need to know in short order what they are reading and why they should continue. Suspense is a virtue with mystery novels—but not for any other kind of writing.

In your first draft, an introduction might be something

like, "Our university needs to upgrade the dormitories. They need paint. The dorms are cold in the winter. The facilities are not environmentally friendly. The university should invest money to make this better." These are not the worst sentences ever written. Each has a subject and a verb. The thesis is clear. But would you be eager to read the rest of this eighteen-page report? Does the language evoke the conditions in the dormitories as vividly as possible?

In contrast, consider the opening paragraph of a recent *New York Times Magazine* piece on child poverty.

> She wakes to the sound of breathing. The smaller children lie tangled beside her, their chests rising and falling under winter coats and wool blankets. A few feet away, their mother and father sleep near the mop bucket they use as a toilet. Two other children share a mattress by the rotting wall where the mice live, opposite the baby, whose crib is warmed by a hair dryer perched on a milk crate."[1]

This may be a hard piece to read because of the content, but you can tell from the introduction that the writing will be shockingly evocative.

Consider this introduction from a story in *The Economist* about the possibility of US support for Taiwan causing a military conflict with China:

> Rousing music accompanies the H-6K, a hulking Chinese bomber, as it sweeps up into a pink sky. Moments later, its

pilot presses a red button, with the panache and fortitude that only a People's Liberation Army (PLA) officer could muster, and a missile streaks towards the island of Guam. The ground ripples and a fiery explosion consumes America's Andersen Air Force Base. Never mind that the PLA propaganda film released in September pinches footage from Hollywood blockbusters; the message is that this is what America can expect if it is foolhardy enough to intervene on behalf of Taiwan in a regional war."[2]

Your introduction is the sales pitch for the rest of the document. I worked in door-to-door sales when I was in college. A friend and I operated a driveway-sealing business. We secured new clients by ringing doorbells during the dinner hour in subdivisions with houses that had asphalt driveways. From the moment the door opened, we needed to be succinct and strategic as we pitched our business. We introduced ourselves as college students, explained our services, and pointed out driveways in the neighborhood that we had recently sealed. That was typically two or three well-constructed sentences. If the person who opened the door was interested, we would explain more: prices, materials, and so on. But if our pitch did not land in those first ten seconds, we were done. The homeowner would say, "Sorry, I'm not interested." By then, the door was swinging shut.

If your introduction is dense, confusing, or uninteresting, a prospective reader will shut the door on you, too. This is especially important for presentations. You do not want the first thirty seconds to signal to your audience that the next half hour will be a boring, meandering mess.

A good introduction must also encapsulate the balance of the document. By the end of the introduction, usually only a paragraph or two, the reader must know what this document is about, including a summary of your recommendations or call to action. If you give your boss a seven-page memo, and she is still wondering what the point of it is after five pages, you have failed as a writer. There is an old newspaper expression—*"Don't bury the lede"*—which means that you should not put essential information far down in the story (e.g., which team won the game). Journalists are taught that the opening sentences of an article should offer the *who*, *where*, *what*, and *why* of a story. The subsequent paragraphs are for filling in the details. With a presentation, the lede can be something as simple as, "I'm here today to persuade you that we ought to legalize marijuana in our state."

That will prevent audience members whispering to one another ten minutes into your talk, "Do you know what he's talking about or why he's here?"

"Not yet, but he seems very interested in drugs and criminals."

Susan Cain, author of the book *Quiet: The Power of Introverts in a World That Can't Stop Talking*, has a wonderful introduction to her TED talk. She tells an amusing but poignant story about arriving at summer camp with a suitcase full of books, only to have her counselor gather the girls together and teach them a cheer that they would do every day all summer. "And it went like this," Cain says. "'R-O-W-D-I-E, that's the way we spell rowdie. Rowdie, rowdie, let's get rowdie.'"* Later, when Cain was finally able to escape with a book, the concerned counselor explained the importance of camp spirit and urged her to be more outgoing. So, she tried to pass as an extrovert—then, and in many future personal and professional settings.

Cain's story brilliantly captures the discomfort of being an introvert in an extrovert's world. She finishes her introduction with a clear and compelling thesis: "Now this is what many introverts do, and it's our loss for sure, but it is also our colleagues' loss and our communities' loss. And at the risk of sounding grandiose, it is the world's loss. Because when it comes to creativity and to leadership, we need introverts doing what they do best."[3] Anyone listening to the first few minutes of this talk knows exactly what it will be about, and also that Susan Cain will be interesting and engaging as she elaborates on her thesis.

Someone once told me that Jimmy Carter routinely tore the first page off all memos and threw the rest in the trash can. I have heard the same story told about Lyndon Johnson. I suspect both stories are apocryphal, or at least exaggerated. Still, there is a lesson: the important stuff should be summarized at the beginning. Also, if the introduction is interesting enough, the reader may not throw the rest of what you have written in the trash.

---

* The correct spelling is r-o-w-d-y, which makes the story even funnier.

16. Use the active voice.

*The human brain absorbs ideas most easily when
they are expressed in the active voice; the passive
voice creates distance from the reader.*

Compare the following sentences:

Jane hit her boss on the head with a canoe paddle.
The boss of Jane was hit on the head by a paddle used for
canoeing.

Obviously, I have made the second sentence as awful as possible. I did that by using the passive voice, which is a terrific tool for producing awful sentences. The brain processes active and passive sentences differently. According to an article in the *Personality and Social Psychology Bulletin*, the content of a passage feels more psychologically distant when it is written in the passive voice.[4] For example, in one experiment participants were divided randomly into two groups. The first group was asked to read a passage written in the active voice about a proposed trip to France. The second group read *the same content* composed in the passive voice. The passive voice made the trip seem further in the future.

The passive voice also shifts the focus of a sentence. Consider: *The quick brown fox jumped over the lazy dog.* That sentence, in the active voice, is about the fox. Now look at the passive version. *The lazy dog was jumped over by the quick brown fox*. This sentence is about the lazy dog. This is not necessarily a trivial point. One expert has warned that writing about rape in the passive voice (the woman was raped) can redirect blame onto the victim and away from the perpetrator (he raped the woman).

Sometimes writers deliberately try to distance themselves from their prose with the passive voice. Academics, for example, tend to project objectivity by using phrases like "It is commonly believed..." This is one reason academic writing tends to be turbid and offputting. (Also, academics use words like turbid and offputting.) Politicians use the passive voice when they are trying to avoid accountability, such as the famously pathetic phrase, "Mistakes were made." That sentence places attention on the mistakes rather than on the person who made them. "I made mistakes" is a more fulsome apology because it directs attention to the person accepting responsibility.

The active voice is more likely to engage your readers with the material. It literally draws them in. Active sentences also focus on the subject of a sentence, which is usually your intent. Of course, if you are trying to distance yourself from a situation in which you have made mistakes, the passive voice might be just what you need.

17. Use organizational techniques, such as subheadings, numbering, and bullet points, to lead the reader through your text.

Formatting offers signposts to help the reader absorb your most important points.

The reader is your customer. Your job is to make the reading experience user-friendly, as if you were a tour guide leading the reader through your document:

Ladies and gentlemen, if you look straight ahead, you'll see my thesis. Let's pause here for a moment, because this is the big idea that I really want you to absorb. Got that? Okay, let's move along as I point out supporting evidence for my thesis. On the right, you'll see compelling results from a recent study. On the left, there is a clever example you won't soon forget. Finally, just before we get to the gift shop, we'll pause again so I can restate my thesis and make clear what I expect you to do next.

One benefit of word processing is that you have tools— boldface, bullets, color—that can be used to provide a visual tour for the reader. For example, you can highlight your thesis by putting it in bold, or by making the font bigger, or by putting it in a box at the top of the page. Your formatting is saying: **Look here.**

If you have a series of ideas that might get lost in a long, cumbersome paragraph, use numbers or bullets instead. For example, if I were running for president of the Wheelan family, here are three immediate changes I might promise:

1. Dessert will be served *before* every meal. (Notice the italics to add emphasis.)
2. The dog will walk himself.
3. I will throw the chore board in the trash!

A discerning reader may be skeptical of my platform, but the three-point plan is easy to understand. If you have a longer document, you can use formatting to lead the reader through it, just like signage for passengers getting off a flight and looking for the baggage claim. Your title will summarize the whole document. Each section will have a subheading that further explains the progression of your case:

The Case for Transferable Commercial Fishing Licenses

1. Introduction: A Better Way to Protect Our Fisheries
2. How the Status Quo Contributes to Overfishing
3. My Plan: Transferable Licenses to Limit the Catch
4. Evidence in Support of My Plan
5. Why We Must Act Now

No one is going to have difficulty understanding the structure of that memo. I teach a class on education policy in which we read an excellent report from the Wallace Foundation on effective school principals. This is a twenty-five-page document packed with detailed observations and research. The beginning of the report has five bullet points that summarize the role of effective principals:

This Wallace Perspective is a culling of our lessons to describe what it is that effective principals do. In short, we believe they perform five key practices well:[5]

- Shaping a vision of academic success for all students
- Creating a climate hospitable to education
- Cultivating leadership in others
- Improving instruction
- Managing people, data, and processes to foster school improvement

My students can skip the full report and get the gist of it from those five bullet points. I do not endorse this academic shortcut, but I do applaud the Wallace Foundation for making it possible.

After admonishing his cabinet members to write shorter memos, Winston Churchill offered them four suggestions for doing so. He numbered them: i, ii, iii, iv. Churchill went so far as to say that if a document is well formatted with headings and subheadings, the rest of the content could be discarded. This was point iii: "Often the occasion is best met by submitting not a full-dress Report, but an *Aide-mémoire* consisting of headings only, which can be expanded orally if needed."

Let's take a small detour to consider the subfield of engineering called human-centered design. The point of human-centered design, or "design thinking," is to make products as easy and convenient for consumers as possible. The design thinkers are the ones who put cup holders in cars and wheels on suitcases. (Remarkably, I grew up without the benefit of either.) These were not innovations made possible by technological breakthroughs. No team of scientists discovered how to put wheels on a suitcase. Someone just had to think, "Wouldn't it be easier if there were wheels on the bottom?" Similarly, a cup holder is a lot less technologically advanced than a car's engine, but it took a half century for someone to figure out that motorists might be safer and more comfortable if they did not have to balance hot coffee between their legs.

The questions at the heart of human-centered design are always the same: How will the consumer interact with this product or situation? How can we make that experience better? Once you envision the reader as your customer, you can design reader-friendly features, such as executive summaries, overviews, sidebars, and other tools that make what you are writing more digestible. Some readers will skim what you write; others will glance only at the first page. You can design a document that highlights—perhaps literally—the most important points so that even a casual reader will get them. For example, your twelve-page memo urging your company (a chain of delicatessens) to switch to sustainably sourced tuna might have a shaded box on the first page:

THE BIG IDEA: IF WE SWITCH TO SUSTAINABLY SOURCED TUNA, WE WILL GAIN CUSTOMERS IN STORES WITH A HIGH PROPORTION OF AFFLUENT, COLLEGE-EDUCATED CONSUMERS.

Even a coworker who tosses your memo in the recycling bin is likely to absorb the key point.

I stated earlier that I sometimes take the student papers with long, dense blocks of text and slide them to the back of the pile. Which papers do I pick up first? The ones formatted in ways that make me excited to pick them up. It is the writing equivalent of putting wheels on a suitcase.

18. Avoid useless words and phrases.

If a word or phrase can be removed ~~easily~~ without changing the content in a ~~really~~ meaningful way, take it out.

Unnecessary words get in the way of clear, succinct writing. They slow the reader down and draw attention away from the words that matter. There is an irony here: shorter sentences often pack more punch. Here is an example:

He hit me very hard in the head, and I began bleeding profusely everywhere.

This sentence is full of words that need to come out. The modifier "very" adds nothing to the observation that you have been hit hard in the head. Also, if you are bleeding profusely, then "everywhere" is redundant.

He hit me hard in the head, and I began bleeding profusely.

This sentence is better, but there is room to be more succinct. If you begin bleeding profusely, then it is obvious you were hit "hard," so that word can come out, too.

He hit me in the head, and I began bleeding.

The third sentence is the most jarring, and arguably the most effective. The descriptor "profusely" adds something, but if you are aiming for brevity (as Winston Churchill would like you to do), then it can come out. The point of the sentence is that someone has just hit you hard enough to make you bleed. That will grab the reader's attention; if you can do it in ten words instead of twelve, so much the better.

Good editors have a keen eye for the unnecessary. Once you have finished your first draft, you are now an editor. Here are the kinds of words and phrases you should purge:

In my opinion . . . You're the one writing the piece, so who else's opinion would it be?

Obviously . . . If it is obvious, why are you pointing it out?

Needless to say . . . Then why are you saying it?

Indeed ... I have no idea why this word exists.

Some people might say ... Who?

It goes without saying ... Then you don't need to say it.

No offense, but ... This is an indication that you are about to write or say something offensive.

Very ... This word is meant to magnify but typically has the opposite effect. Which of these sentences is stronger: "He is very stupid." Or "He is stupid." The latter sentence feels more forthright.

Quite ... The same as very, only worse.

Later I will qualify this advice. There might be a reason for some of these phrases to creep back into your writing. For now, they are superfluous words that will not be missed when they are gone. When I wrote for *The Economist*, I emailed my stories from Chicago to an editor in London. The edited piece came back to me a few hours later. More often than not, I could not discern at first glance what had been changed—yet somehow the story seemed better and the word count had been cut by 10 or 15 percent. Only when I studied the piece closely did I realize what was different: unnecessary words were gone; redundant sentences were cut; a long quote was trimmed down to its punchiest part. The editing was so skillful that the piece was shorter, better, and still entirely in the spirit of what I had originally filed.

Sometimes more than a stray word needs to be cut. Taking out a redundant sentence can leave a paragraph tighter and stronger. Maybe a whole paragraph needs to go. When I was working on the second draft of this book, I cut a thousand words in a twenty-minute stretch.

Good editing is a win-win: the piece gets shorter *and* better.

19. Every argument should be supported by evidence or analysis; the more specific, the better.

*If you say something is true, you need to give
the reader a reason to believe you.*

Writing is about building a case, whether you are trying to get a refund for a canceled vacation rental or preparing articles of impeachment against the president of the United States. Your case is built on a foundation of arguments; each argument must be substantiated, or else the case will collapse. To put it more succinctly, you have asserted things to be true: Why should the rest of us believe you? Any significant assertion should be supported by data, testimony from an expert, study results, an example, or some other evidence from a credible source that validates your claim.

Which of the following arguments is more compelling?

Michael Jordan is the greatest basketball player of all time. Everybody knows that.

Michael Jordan is the greatest basketball player of all time. He won six NBA championships. He was selected MVP of the league five times. He won ten scoring titles and was selected to the All-Star team fourteen times.

Perhaps you believe that Lebron James is a better player than Michael Jordan was. If so, you are going to have to put some data against that assertion. I believe Jordan was better, and here is my evidence: Lebron is 4–6 in NBA Finals series, whereas Jordan was a perfect 6–0.

The information you use to validate your arguments needs to come from a source the reader will consider authoritative. If we are still evaluating NBA players, The National Association of Basketball Writers is a better source than "a loud guy I met at a local sports bar who seems to know a lot about basketball." An oncologist at a major university hospital is more credible with regard to cancer risks than a blogger who has watched a lot of YouTube videos.

A credible source must also be objective, meaning that the party you are leaning on for corroboration does not have a stake in the outcome of what is being discussed. When it comes to climate change, for example, the Intergovernmental Panel on Climate Change, the United Nations body responsible for assessing climate-related science, is a better source than ExxonMobil, since the latter has a financial incentive to downplay the harms associated with fossil fuels. During the 1980s and early 1990s, an organization called the Council on Tobacco Research consistently cast doubt on the public health consensus that smoking causes cancer. Who or what was this seemingly august group pushing back on decades of peer-reviewed research? Remarkably, the Council on Tobacco Research was an organization funded by the tobacco industry with the mission of promoting tobacco use and protecting the industry from regulation. No reasonable person, let alone professional journalists, should have considered this entity a legitimate source, yet their official-sounding reports and "experts" sowed confusion on the harms of smoking. When the major American tobacco companies entered into a legal settlement with forty-six state attorneys-general in 1998, the Council on Tobacco Research was disbanded as part of the agreement.

A good source is knowledgeable, honest, and objective. Most important, the reader needs to think, "Yes, I believe that." At the same time, you are trying to build your case as efficiently as possible. Just as the best building materials are strong but light, the best supporting evidence is compelling but concise. Here is the clever way *The Economist* documented the claim that many Americans are moving out of urban areas as a result of Covid: "MoveBuddha, a relocation website, says that searches for places in New York's suburbs are up almost 250% compared with this time last year."[6] In one sentence, that factoid supports the assertion that the pandemic caused a major shift in where people are choosing to live.

In an article in *The Atlantic* provocatively entitled, "How American Health Care Killed My Father," David Goldhill describes how infections acquired in the hospital are deadly but preventable. Here is how he compellingly expresses the scale of that problem: "My dad became a statistic—merely one of the roughly 100,000 Americans whose deaths are caused or influenced by infections picked up in hospitals. One hundred thousand deaths: more than double the number of people killed in car crashes, five times the number killed in homicides, 20 times the total number of our armed forces killed in Iraq and Afghanistan. Another victim in a building American tragedy."[7] Those sixty-seven words put a lot of heft behind his thesis.

Again, think of a legal analogy. A lawyer cannot assert, "My client was not at the scene of the crime" without offering corroborating evidence. *Okay, where was your client?* We want to see video footage or hear testimony from someone who was with him. Sometimes I will comment on student policy memos, "I want this idea to work, but I'm not persuaded it will." The memos are meant to build a case for a policy change (e.g., a waiting period for buying a gun to reduce suicides) but there is not sufficient evidence to convince me that the policy will have its intended effect. The students aren't wrong necessarily; I'm just not persuaded they're right.

Nothing persuades a reader like good evidence.

20. Use appendices for supporting material that is relevant but might interrupt the flow of your document.

An appendix is a separate section, often at
the end of a memo or report, that provides
detailed or technical information that will be
of interest to some readers but not others.

Mae West, a provocative actress and sex symbol in the first half of the twentieth century, once said, "Too much of a good thing can be wonderful." Mae West was also a writer, but I doubt this quote was in reference to her writing. *Because too many good words on the page are rarely a wonderful thing.* Strong writing requires two things that are in tension: substance and brevity. On the one hand, great writers inject their work with details, stories, and supporting evidence. On the other hand, good writing is succinct and does not waste the time of the reader. Appendices are a helpful tool for striking that balance.

An appendix is typically used to provide additional information on a topic that may interest some readers but not others. Anyone who wants to know all the steps for getting a new drug approved by the FDA can read Appendix Q. Others will be content to know that the FDA has a process but will have no interest in reading the gritty details that have been relegated to the appendix. Your writing can use an appendix to offer readers that choice: "For a more complete description of the steps in the FDA drug approval process, see Appendix Q."

Yes, Churchill was a fan of appendices. Here is his second point for achieving brevity: "If a report relies on detailed analysis of some complicated factors, or on statistics, these should be set out in an Appendix." Since I have referred so often to Churchill's memo on writing memos, I have included the whole document in Appendix A. (I hope you appreciate that I have used an appendix to include a document making a case for appendices!)

Footnotes are also a good tool for offering short pieces of information that do not fit neatly in the body of the document. In general, footnotes should not be more than a sentence or two; longer passages should be made into appendices.

Whether you choose a footnote or appendix, the motivation is the same: this is information some readers might find interesting but putting it in the body of the document would be more disruptive than helpful.

21. Acknowledge the costs or limitations of what you are proposing.

Nothing in life is perfect. Strong writing anticipates reasonable objections and concerns.

Writing and speaking are often intended to persuade. The goal is to transform skeptics into supporters so that they will give you a job, support your candidate, invest in your business, or otherwise buy what you are selling (literally or figuratively). You cannot accomplish this by hiding the limitations of your case. Rather, you should acknowledge the costs or shortcomings of what you are pitching while persuading readers that they should still be supportive. Most proposals are like prescription drugs: they are not flawless; we just expect to be persuaded that the benefits outweigh the harms.

Imagine that you have hired Taylor Swift to play a concert in your backyard to celebrate your daughter's fifth birthday. The neighbors are concerned that the concert will cause chaos: noise, traffic, unwanted media attention. If you can afford to hire Taylor Swift to play a private party, we'll assume that your neighbors are influential people who take their properties seriously. If you were to compose a letter in response to concerns raised by the neighborhood association, which opening do you think would likely get the best response?

1. I am writing to refute your ridiculous and unfounded concerns about Marigold's fifth birthday party.
2. I am writing to let you know that I understand and appreciate your concerns about the noise and traffic that may result from Marigold's birthday concert. I have taken several steps to mitigate any potential problems.

The answer is number two, according to the science of persuasion. In fields ranging from marriage counseling to peace negotiations, we have learned that the most effective way to address disagreement is by validating the concerns of others, not by ridiculing or ignoring them. This does not mean that you *agree* with the protestations; it means you have listened to them and can articulate what they are. Experts even advise repeating them back: "What I'm hearing you say is that having a Taylor Swift concert in my backyard for eighty-five of Marigold's closest friends might cause a lot of noise and traffic." Human psychology is such that we are most open to compromise or changing our views when we believe that the other party understands and respects us. In contrast, if we perceive that someone is not listening to our concerns, or is treating them as illegitimate—"You must hate Marigold, birthday parties, and Taylor Swift!"— then the most common reaction is to dig deeper into an entrenched position.

My students and I once had the good fortune to meet with

Bertie Ahern, who had been the taoiseach (prime minister) of Ireland during the negotiations mentioned earlier that brought peace to Northern Ireland. Ahern represented the Republic of Ireland in those complicated talks, which included the British government, representatives of Catholic groups sympathetic to the Irish Republican Army, and representatives of Protestant groups that also had militant wings. What struck me about Ahern's description of his participation in the negotiations was how much time he spent trying to figure out ways for *the other parties* to get what they needed. Yes, he was representing Ireland, but Ireland would only benefit if the talks succeeded, and the talks would only succeed if the others around the table came out ahead, too.

A more prosaic reason to alert readers to the flaws or limitations of what you are proposing is: if you don't, someone else will. That will make you appear naïve, deceitful, or insensitive for having glossed over a reasonable objection. Remember, you are not pitching perfection; you are pitching an improvement on the status quo. Most prescription drugs have long lists of side effects; yet for many people, taking the medicine is much better than not taking the medicine. If you point out the costs or limitations of what you are writing about, it will inoculate you from the criticism of others.

> Yes, the plan is expensive, but doing nothing will be far
> more expensive in the long run.
> True, he can't hit a curveball, but he's getting better at that
> every season and he's a great infielder.
> No, this health care plan will not improve outcomes for

those without insurance, but it will reduce costs signifi-
cantly for those who do have insurance.

We do not expect our business to be profitable in year one,
but even our most conservative models suggest we will
be cash-flow positive by year three.

Yes, what you read in the newspapers is true, but I have
completed an anger management program.

The New Yorker recently ran an article on a nonprofit group
called the Fortune Society that helps former inmates rein-
tegrate into society.[8] One of the challenges for ex-convicts is
explaining a prison sentence to a prospective employer. The
wrong thing to do is to pretend that it did not happen. Most
employers run a background check that will expose a criminal
conviction. The Fortune Society conducts mock job interviews
in which former inmates practice answering open-ended
questions like "What else should I know?" or "If we do a background check, is there anything that will come up?"

The ideal answer is something like: "Yes, when I was
younger and behaving stupidly, an unfortunate situation
occurred, and someone got badly hurt.* This led to my becoming involved in the criminal-justice system. But I studied
hard and attended several programs while I was in jail. That
person I was is not who I am now." The point is to put the best
face on a previous failure, not to pretend that it did not happen. We can all learn from that.

The best way to get what you want is by showing other

---

* Note the deliberate and effective use of the passive voice here!

people that it will help them, too, or at least not hurt them. Let them know that you have heard their concerns. Do not oversell yourself or what you are pitching. And, if possible, invite the neighbors to Marigold's birthday party; if they get to attend the Taylor Swift concert, they are less likely to complain about it.

22. Show, don't tell.

Any point you make will be amplified
by vivid, memorable examples.

Examples are fun to read or listen to. They also tend to stick with the reader and put a finer point on your analysis. (Remember Susan Cain doing the R-O-W-D-I-E cheer at summer camp?) The best examples are rich in details that speak for themselves. Consider a profile of former New York governor Andrew Cuomo in *The New Yorker* by Nick Paumgarten.[9] Cuomo was forced to resign in 2021 over allegations of sexual harassment; Paumgarten's article came out a year before that and suggested that Cuomo was not the hero his supporters were making him out to be. Paumgarten begins by describing Governor Cuomo as someone willing to go to great lengths to win a political battle. That is telling, not showing, and it is not particularly persuasive. But then he relates a story from the 1982 New York State Democratic Convention *to show* how Machiavellian Andrew Cuomo can be. At the time, Andrew Cuomo's father, Mario, was running for governor against New York City mayor Ed Koch. Both the Cuomo and Koch campaigns were aggressively lobbying the convention delegates on behalf of their candidates. Here is the vignette from Paumgarten's *New Yorker* story:

> On the day of the state convention, in Syracuse, as Cuomo's campaign tried to bluff its way into having enough delegates to stay in the race, Andrew had a staffer charter a pleasure boat (and then have it conk out in the middle of the Onondaga Lake) to sequester a bunch of Cuomo-leaning delegates, so that Koch's campaign couldn't court them.

Andrew Cuomo deliberately engineered a boat breakdown in the middle of a lake to gain political advantage for his father! Once you have read that, you won't think of Andrew Cuomo the same way again. And you will not forget the story. That is showing, not telling.

Consider another political example. In 1992, Bill Clinton, then governor of Arkansas, was running for president. He left the campaign trail to return to Arkansas to oversee the execution of Ricky Ray Rector, who had been convicted of killing two men, including a police officer. The death penalty is always controversial, but this case had two additional layers of controversy. First, Governor Clinton was accused of political grandstanding for flying back to Arkansas for the execution; attending it was not legally necessary. Second, Ricky Ray Rector had severely limited cognitive capacity. When he was apprehended by police for the murders, he shot himself in the temple and did serious brain damage. This created a legal complication: Was

Ricky Ray Rector sufficiently mentally competent to face execution?

The US Supreme Court had ruled in *Ford v. Wainwright* that for capital punishment to be constitutional: (1) A convicted criminal must be capable of comprehending that he is going to be put to death; and (2) He must understand why the sentence has been imposed. Thus, it was legally necessary to determine if Ricky Ray Rector had the mental capacity to understand what was happening to him. If he did not, the State of Arkansas could not execute him.

At trial, many experts testified about Rector's mental capacity: his IQ, the nature of his brain injury, and so on. But decades later, one detail from that case has stuck with me. *When Ricky Ray Rector was offered his last meal before being led to the execution chamber, he asked if he could set aside his pecan pie to eat later.*[10] There are a lot of ways to express that a person does not have the capacity to understand capital punishment. That is a powerful one.

Robert M. Gates served as the US secretary of defense for two presidents, George W. Bush and Barack Obama. Secretary Gates often emphasized the responsibility that rests on the shoulders of the person who sends American soldiers into combat knowing that some of them will be killed. This is the emotional toll that comes with the job. But the phrase "emotional toll" is abstract; it is telling, not showing. It does not give the reader a sense of what it feels like to be in the shoes of the secretary of defense. Fortunately, Robert Gates is a compelling writer. In a foreword he wrote for a book on political reform, Gates *shows* readers what it feels like to hold that job. Each morning, he was given a list of every American soldier who had been killed in combat during the preceding twenty-four hours. Here is Gates's description of what he did with that list:

> Simply signing a condolence letter didn't seem enough, so each night during my tenure—more than four and a half years—as the secretary of defense, I wrote handwritten messages to the loved ones of these service members. And every night as I wrote those notes, I wept.[11]

Now do you feel the weight of that job? Does the vision of him weeping as he writes evoke a different response than the phrase "emotional toll"?

There is one other thing worth pointing out about Secretary Gates's handwritten notes: the "why." Secretary Gates was writing to the bereaved families of fallen soldiers to assure them that their loved ones were not mere statistics. To do that, he needed to write the notes by hand. A form letter can be printed in bulk, but a handwritten note from the secretary is an indication that every soldier matters. It cannot be mass-produced. The content of those letters was arguably less important than the fact that Defense Secretary Robert Gates took the time to write each one of them.

The powerful vision of Secretary Gates writing those letters and weeping—every night for four and a half years—is why we aspire to show rather than to tell.

23. Offer an ending that will persuade and inspire.

Make your ending count by reminding your audience of your thesis and inviting action, if appropriate.

Your final words are your closing argument. As in a courtroom, it is your chance to reaffirm your case and advocate for the outcome you are seeking. The conclusion should remind readers or listeners why they got this far. It should encapsulate the thesis in a way that resonates emotionally. If there is a call to action—to urge people to vote, to give money, to invest, to protest, to clean up after their dogs, or to do something else—this is your final chance to make that plea explicit.

The introduction and conclusion are the bookends. The introduction urges people to stick with you; the conclusion reminds them why they did. One effective tool is to have your ending "call back" to your beginning. Tell us the woeful story of a mother on welfare at the beginning, then finish by telling us about how she got a job after the 1996 welfare reform. At a minimum, restate your thesis emphatically. Earlier you read a summary (in bullet points) of a report called *School Principal as Leader: Guiding Schools to Better Teaching and Learning*. The thesis of that relatively long report is that effective principals are the key to good schools. Here is the conclusion, which reminds the reader of the thesis one final time:

> We still have a lot to learn, but we have already learned a great deal. In the face of this growing body of knowledge and experience, it is clear that now is the time to step up efforts to strengthen school leadership. Without effective principals, the national goal we've set of transforming failing schools will be next to impossible to achieve. But with an effective principal in every school comes promise.

Nelson Mandela had an extraordinary life. His autobiography, published in 1994, is titled *Long Walk to Freedom*. The book describes Mandela's early life under apartheid in South Africa, his twenty-seven years in prison, and his eventual election as president. *Long Walk to Freedom* was published at the beginning of Mandela's presidential term. South Africa had finally given political representation to its Black majority, but a tremendous amount of work lay ahead as the nation sought to repair the historical damage done to its minority populations and to provide economic opportunity for all. How does one end a book like that?

The broad thesis of Mandela's six-hundred-page book was that the long walk to freedom had been extraordinary—but it was not over. Here is the final paragraph:

> I have walked that long walk to freedom. I have tried not to falter; I have made many missteps along the way. But I

have discovered the secret that after climbing a great hill, one only finds that there are many more hills to climb. I have taken a moment here to rest, to steal a view of the glorious vista that surrounds me, to look back on the distance I have come. But I can rest only for a moment, for with freedom come responsibilities, and I dare not linger, for my walk is not yet ended.[12]

Mandela gives us a sense of the whole book in one final uplifting paragraph. The reader is reminded of the extraordinary mountain Mandela has climbed, but also of the challenges South Africa had yet to confront. The conclusion captures the tone of the book: optimistic but not naïve. The sentences feel familiar but not repetitive to a reader who has come to the end of this long story. In short, Mandela used the conclusion to put an elegant bow on a brilliant book.

Sometimes I get to the end of a student paper and I worry that a page has been lost. The analysis ends without any effective wrap-up, like a dinner guest who gets up abruptly from the table and walks out the door. This is a wasted opportunity. When called to present a closing argument, no decent lawyer ever says, "That's all I have. The jury has probably heard enough."

Give us your thesis one last time in a way that will stick with us.

24. Edit like you've never edited before.

Editing is the process by which imperfect but well-organized writing is refined into something better.

For me, this is the fun part. When you begin the editing process, you feel like someone who has just climbed out of bed. By the end, you are dressed in designer clothes, bedecked in jewelry, and smelling of fine cologne. The writing has become tighter and punchier. Your arguments are clearer and more forceful. The clunky sentences are gone, and the examples feel just right. The introduction and conclusion are compelling bookends for your polished prose. With a speech, this means that you're ready to stand up and say it out loud.

Good editing requires doing the things described in this section over and over again. My stories for *The Economist* typically went through eight or ten drafts, and that was before I sent them to London for formal editing. Editing is not a one-shot deal. It is a process that you repeat until there are no more improvements to be made. Your drafts should get shorter as you cut unnecessary words and sentences. However, editing may also identify places where injecting an anecdote will allow you to show rather than tell. There is nothing wrong with cutting in some places and adding in others. Although the structure of your piece should have been functional before you began writing, this is the last chance to fix any structural problems. For example, I noticed in revising this book that two recommendations overlapped. I combined them into one. Sometimes you do have to pay the contractor to move a load-bearing wall.

I am not a big reader of gossip magazines, but once in a while when I glance at *Us Weekly* in the checkout line at the grocery story there is a headline like, "Stars Who Are Completely Unrecognizable Without Makeup." (It's not just women, by the way.) Here is one real headline: "18 Photos of Makeup-Wearing Male Celebs Without Their Makeup On."[13] The point is that the celebrity photos in those articles do not look like the photos of those same celebrities when they show up on the red carpet at the Oscars. Why? Because celebrities work hard to get ready for the red carpet. According to a stylist interviewed for *Marie Claire*, getting a celebrity "red carpet ready" takes roughly a month.[14]

Let's go back to Supreme Court Justice Elena Kagan, or more specifically Elena Kagan's mother, who apparently demanded excellent editing from her children. Justice Kagan explained to a University of Wisconsin audience in 2017, "My mother's voice is in my head all the time. And writing was important to Gloria Kagan. She'd go over her children's papers with them, sentence by sentence, pressing them to make improvements."[15] I suspect that Justice Kagan's first drafts are inelegant, just like ours are, but we never see those drafts. When we read Elena Kagan's writing, it is likely to be the fifth or eighth draft, after she has done the editing that her mother expected.

Editing is the process of getting your writing ready for the red carpet. It takes work, but you will see wonderful results.

BUFFING AND POLISHING

25. Insert graphics and photos that support your analysis.

Visual images are powerful complements to your text.

The old saying goes, "A picture is worth a thousand words." Sometimes that is literally true. A photo can pack more emotional punch than a written description. For example, video and still photos from the Vietnam War are credited with bringing the war into the living rooms of Americans and turning public opinion against that conflict. One particular image was described by the *New York Times* on the fiftieth anniversary of its publication as "a photo that changed the course of the Vietnam War."[1] Associated Press photographer Eddie Adams captured the image of the national police chief of South Vietnam shooting a handcuffed Vietcong prisoner in the head. The photo ran on the front page of newspapers across America. It is a horrible, horrible image—which is why it changed minds about the war. "It hit people in the gut in a way that only a visual text can do," history professor Michelle Nickerson explains in the *New York Times* article.

The execution captured by the photo was likely a violation of the Geneva Conventions. The shooter was an official in a government supported by the United States. According to the *New York Times* analysis, "Adams's photo made people question whether the United States was fighting for a just cause." *Just one photo.*

Photos are typically copyrighted by the person who took them. Not only will you need to give credit for the image, but you may also need to pay a royalty and get permission from the owner of the copyright. Photos and images that are in the "public domain" can be used free; this means that the copyright has lapsed or that the owner has donated his or her work to the public domain. Creative Commons is a nonprofit organization that seeks to make creative work available to the public at no cost.[2] These items are marked with some variation of the Creative Commons license: (cc). Each Creative Commons mark denotes a different allowable use: public use in any format with no conditions; commercial use with attribution; noncommercial use with attribution; and so on.

Another way to sidestep any copyright issues is to use your own images.

I did not include the Vietnam War photo described above in part because I would have had to pay a hefty licensing fee. Also, the photo is so disturbingly graphic—the reason it changed minds about the Vietnam War—that it would be inappropriate for readers who are interested in better writing, not the brutalities of war. The purpose of this book (#1!) is to teach writing, not to relitigate US military involvement in Southeast Asia.

Graphics are a related tool that can convey data more effectively than raw numbers. The pie chart below shows the breakdown of gun deaths in the United States. What leaps out from the graphic is that suicides account for most gun deaths in America, even though homicides tend to get more attention. Mass shootings, including school shootings, make up a tiny slice of firearm deaths. I could have given you the percentage breakdown for all those categories, but the graphic expresses the relative magnitudes of different kinds of firearm deaths more starkly.

Deaths from Firearms in the United States, 2019

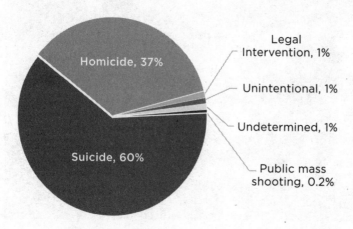

This pie chart does an excellent job of illustrating the frequency of different kinds of gun deaths, particularly the prevalence of suicides relative to mass shootings. Source: UC Davis Health: https://health.ucdavis.edu/what-you-can-do/facts.html.

In other cases, an image may simply break up a thousand words so that a dense block of text does not scare off the reader. This is the reason that newspapers, magazines, and web pages are packed with photos and images. The photo below ran with an article in the *New York Times* about programs to help students who fell behind during the pandemic.[3] The article was packed with analysis, facts, and figures. The picture of students getting off a school bus will not win a Pulitzer Prize, but it does make the article more inviting.

Visual images can be powerful, or at least pleasantly distracting. They are jewelry for your writing.

This photo accompanied an article in the *New York Times* about summer school for students who fell behind during Covid. Images make serious writing more reader-friendly. Cornell Watson, *New York Times*.

26. Interject the voices and emotions of the people you are writing about.

Quotations will make your analysis more
vivid and interesting; they can also inject
voices dissimilar from your own.

One way to show rather than tell is by letting characters speak for themselves. You can explain that Jack was nervous on the first day of class. Or you can quote Jack: "On the first day of class, I rushed out of the seminar room and puked in the men's room." Jack's exact words tell us more about how he was feeling than my description does, and the quote is more interesting to read, too.

I once found myself stuck in the middle seat on an airplane next to an extremely rude and angry man. As I tried to read the newspaper, this guy began to complain loudly about where I was resting my elbow. He was furious—at me, at the airline, and, based on his broad range of complaints, at much of the world. His tirade became bad enough that I pushed my "call" button to summon the flight attendant. When the flight attendant appeared in the aisle, I realized that describing this guy as a lunatic (telling) might make me look like the crazy one. I had an epiphany: *The flight attendant needs to see this guy's crazy behavior for herself* (showing). I turned to the man and said, "Why don't you explain the problem?" He let loose with a rant so unhinged that the flight attendant escorted him away. His own words were my best evidence (and I was able to move to the aisle seat).

In President Barack Obama's postpresidential autobiography, *A Promised Land*, he makes the case that Republican opposition to the Affordable Care Act was less about the specifics of health care reform and more about sabotaging his presidency. This is a big claim that smacks of partisan complaining. But Obama makes his point by quoting Republican senator Jim DeMint, who told conservative activists on a conference call, "If we're able to stop Obama on this, it will be his Waterloo. It will break him."[4] Those are compelling words—and they come from Jim DeMint, not President Obama.

Quotations are testimony from people with firsthand experience. In the *New Yorker* profile of New York governor Andrew Cuomo that I referred to earlier, author Nick Paumgarten makes the point that Cuomo is not a warm and fuzzy guy. To do that, he offers an anonymous quote from a former aide: "[Cuomo] was born for social distancing." *Ouch*. That is a succinct and scathing line, made more powerful by the fact that it comes from a former ally, not a political opponent.

Quotations can also broaden your writing and presentations by giving voice to people who offer a different perspective. You are one person with one set of life experiences. If you are writing about prison conditions, it is unlikely that you have served time in prison, nor have you worked as a corrections officer. Yet both of these viewpoints are essential if you are going to write or speak meaningfully about creating a prison environment that is humane and safe. One approach would be to interview lots of inmates and prison guards and then summarize what they told you. This is not a terrible approach, but it does filter everything they say through you; the result would be your interpretation of other people's thoughts. This also puts you at risk of "telling" rather than "showing." The alternative, which also happens to be easier in many cases, is to let people speak for themselves by quoting them in your writing, or by sharing video or audio in your presentation.

Broadcast mediums routinely inject relevant voices: podcasts, documentaries, even local news. When a reporter covers a house fire or bank robbery, one essential ingredient of that news-gathering formula is getting local reactions. Why? Because a story is more interesting and accurate if it incorporates the voices of those affected rather than leaning entirely on one person's summary of the event. The National Public Radio program *All Things Considered* was introduced in 1971. The first broadcast included a twenty-three-minute story on a protest in Washington, D.C., against the Vietnam War with numerous interviews of protesters and the police officers confronting them. On the fiftieth anniversary of that first broadcast, Bill Siemering, the first director of programming at National Public Radio, explained the logic of the "sound portrait" that he envisioned for the program: "I wanted to be talking with people, not about them. And I wanted to hear voices that aren't heard generally on the air and to have first-person accounts of these things." Siemering also drafted National Public Radio's first mission statement: "NPR should reflect the diversity of America and let the country hear itself."[5]

Even here, you must tread sensitively. Just because a single person says something—one prisoner, one guard—does not mean that person speaks for all prisoners and guards. This becomes even trickier when the goal is to include the voices of traditionally underrepresented racial and ethnic groups. It is insulting and reductionist to interview one member of the Pima nation and assume that that person speaks for all Pima Indians, let alone all Native Americans. On the other hand, if you are writing about water rights in Scottsdale, Arizona, as I once did, and you don't include any Pima voices, then you are also dropping the ball. With quotations, as with so many other facets of effective communication, accuracy demands discretion. A quotation must be representative of some larger reality (just as an effective anecdote must be consistent with the underlying data). If fifty-three prisoners tell you that conditions are abysmal and one tells you, "I'm really enjoying my stay," you cannot use that quote without making clear that the vast majority of inmates feel differently.

Nor can you take one sentence, or a fragment of a sentence, and use it—*even if someone literally said those words*—if it is inconsistent with the larger conversation. You have an obligation to respect the broader meaning of what someone is telling you. (That said, many public figures who insist that they were "quoted out of context" really just said something stupid that they are trying to walk back.) Responsible journalists and authors interview tens or hundreds of people for stories and then select quotes that most vividly and accurately encapsulate what they have been told.

Meanwhile, you must ensure that you preserve your narrative structure. This is still your document or presentation, and the goal is to advance your thesis, not to string together a series of quotes or videos. Your job is to introduce the voices of others in a way that is consistent with the point or points that you are trying to make.

Quotations can be used properly, or they can be abused. With proper discretion, quotes will persuade the reader, add panache to your prose, and broaden the range of views represented.

27. Use stories to reinforce your key points.

*Stories enliven your writing and speaking
and stick with the audience.*

Stories are not just for young children or people looking to pass time on a long flight. They are fundamental to how humans communicate. Most of us are more moved by stories than we are by data or analysis. Stories reach our emotional core—*they speak to our elephants.*

George Shultz, who died in 2021 at the age of one hundred, served as a cabinet member for three US presidents. He is one of only two Americans to have held four different cabinet-level positions. Before that, he was an economist and dean of the business school at the University of Chicago. When George Shultz turned one hundred, he shared with the

Washington Post a list of the ten most important things he had learned in his career.[6] One of those life lessons was that stories are crucial to successful communication in public life. In the *Post* interview, Shultz described an incident from his time as secretary of state. He had presented the draft of a foreign policy speech to President Ronald Reagan. In the margin next to a key section of the speech, Reagan, who is considered to have been one of the great communicators of all time, wrote, "Story." When Shultz asked him to explain, the president replied, "That's the most important point."

Reagan wanted to make sure that he found a story to help explain that crucial idea in the speech. (Can we pause to acknowledge that George Schultz made his point about the power of stories by telling a story about Ronald Reagan?) President Reagan did not consider stories to be entertainment or filler; he believed them to be an essential tool for engaging his audience and speaking to their emotions, not just their minds. In offering this life lesson, Shultz concluded, "Telling a story, [Reagan] made me understand, helps make your case in a way that no abstraction can: A story builds an emotional bond, and emotional bonds build trust."

When I was with *The Economist*, I wrote an article about an organization that was fighting the expansion of legalized gambling in the United States. This group held a convention in Omaha, Nebraska, that I attended as part of my reporting. The purpose of the convention was to persuade the public that the harms of expanding legalized gambling outweigh the benefits. There were myriad discussions about gambling-related social problems. (One of their clever framing devices was the ABCs of legalized gambling: Addiction, Bankruptcy, and Crime.) There were even breakout sections in which religious leaders read passages from the Bible that they believed spoke to the evils of gambling.

I wrote the article twenty-five years ago. Most of the details of the convention, including all the statistics (and the specific Bible passages), have faded from memory. Yet one story sticks in my mind. A former state police officer spoke about his gambling addiction. While this man was still working as a police officer, he had a gambling problem. He gambled, and he lost—over and over. The nature of the addiction, he explained, was that he always believed he could win his money back. In an effort to dig out from his losses, the officer stole cash from the state police evidence room. His plan was to win enough money to cover his losses and replace the stolen cash before anyone discovered it was missing. He lost that money, too. At that point, the officer was despondent. He had lost his family's savings. He would be fired from the state police when his theft was discovered, and he might face criminal prosecution, too. He decided to kill himself.

The man described to all of us in the audience how he drove his police cruiser to a remote spot where he planned to shoot himself. However, he worried that his body would not be discovered, so he called a fellow officer to leave a message. He dialed the number from a pay phone, expecting to get an answering machine. Instead, he accidentally dialed his home number and one of his children answered. He realized in that moment that he could not kill himself. He drove home and turned himself in. "That's why I'm still here," he finished.

It's a tough story, but that was the point. When the officer was done, there was no one in the audience who did not feel the effects of compulsive gambling on a visceral level. Joseph Stalin supposedly said that when a million people die, it is a statistic, but when one man dies, it is a tragedy. Regardless of whether Stalin ever said that or not, the sentiment is correct. Stories put the humanity in numbers. In my story on gambling expansion, I reported that roughly three million Americans had suffered from a pathological gambling problem at some point in their lives.[7] That is a number likely to bounce off most readers. When I began writing this section of the book, I had to look up that statistic again because I had long since forgotten it. But I remembered the police officer's story.

Stories, quotations, and other anecdotal evidence cannot substitute for data. Your storytelling tools must be consistent with some larger empirical reality. Suppose you were asked to write an evaluation of the quality of education at the Richard M. Nixon College Preparatory Academy. When you visit the school, the principal eagerly introduces you to a Nixon Prep student who has just been accepted by Harvard. "Ernestine embodies everything you need to know about our students," the principal declares. *Not really.* It would be lazy or intellectually dishonest to conclude that Nixon Prep is an excellent school because one student was accepted by Harvard, no matter how impressive Ernestine might be. What about the hundreds of other students? On the other hand, if

Nixon Prep accepts a diverse student body and produces test scores that are consistently in the ninety-seventh percentile, you can breathe life into that dry but important statistic by telling stories about Nixon Prep grads who have gone on to do great things, like Ernestine.

Data speak to our brains; stories speak to our emotions—*our elephants*. The best writing and presentations do both.

28. Make strategic use of titles and subject lines.

*Don't waste an opportunity to tell readers
what they are about to read.*

I am often struck when students turn in excellent memos with titles like "Policy Memo #2" or "Memo on School Finance." The title, like a newspaper headline, is an opportunity to tell the reader what the document is about. Why waste an opportunity to sell your ideas or to provide additional information? No newspaper would run a headline, "Results from Last Night's Game Between the Yankees and Red Sox." Rather, it would be, "Yankees Beat Red Sox 9–8 in Thriller."

A good title or subject line is one more courtesy for your reader. In some cases, it may be all they need—if, for example, all they care about is whether the Yankees won or lost. *The Economist* uses a subheadline (**in bold**) below the headline of every story to give a one or two-sentence synopsis: **Maine's Senate race reflects the declining appeal of bipartisanship** or **The persecution of Xinjiang's Muslims is a crime against humanity. It is part of a worldwide attack on human rights.** The reader knows exactly what these stories will be about. In fact, one could read only the headlines and subheadlines and stay relatively informed about the state of the world.

Ironically, even TED talks have useful titles and subheadings. Susan Cain's talk about being an introvert in a world designed for extroverts—remember R-O-W-D-I-E?—is called "Quiet: The Power of Introverts." The TED site describes it this way: "In a culture where being social and outgoing are prized above all else, it can be difficult, even shameful, to be an introvert. But, as Susan Cain argues in this passionate talk, introverts bring extraordinary talents and abilities to the world, and should be encouraged and celebrated." You have a good sense of what you'll be watching before you hit play.

Much modern communication is by email, making your subject line the equivalent of a headline. Which subject line is most likely to grab your boss's attention as she sips her morning coffee?

1. Plumbing Concern
2. URGENT: Toilets Overflowing into Elevator Lobby!

I think the answer is obvious.

As noted earlier, suspense is a virtue if you are writing murder mysteries. For all other writing, give the reader as much information up front as possible, beginning with the title.

29. Have someone unconnected to the project read your draft.

An outside reader can catch mistakes
and offer meaningful feedback.

How do you know if what you have written is clear and compelling? *Give it to someone and ask.* This is a low-tech but effective way to get feedback that will make your next draft better. Is what you have written clear? Is it persuasive? Is it too long? Do the examples make sense? Are there any embarrassing typos or factual errors? If you are making a case for something—a cause, or a candidate, a legal verdict—is this reader persuaded?

The ideal reader is someone who resembles your audience. If you are working on a manuscript for an economics journal, then have a fellow economist read your draft. If you are writing for a general audience, ask someone who is not an expert on your topic. My wife Leah has read nearly everything I have written for the past thirty years. She catches typos. She flags sentences that could be clearer. She tells me whether something is funny or not. On at least one occasion, she has saved me from getting fired. Late one night many years ago, I composed an email to my boss with a list of grievances. Our third child had just been born. I was sleep-deprived. My boss was a smart, kind man with a tendency to micromanage. I am not someone who likes to be micromanaged, especially when I am tired and cranky. Before I hit send, I asked Leah to read the email. She said, "Don't send this tonight." I reread my draft in the morning and was horrified by my semicoherent rant. I hit delete.

I implore my students to share a draft of their papers with a friend, a partner, or a roommate. I suspect my advice is routinely ignored, perhaps because deadline-driven students do not leave enough time to get feedback and make revisions. They may also be sensitive about sharing their work. In any event, an outside reader would flag many of the problems I encounter when the papers are submitted to me. How else can one explain the memo that began, "One key challenge with pubic education is lack of funding." Spellcheck did not catch that mistake; a roommate might have.

30. Kill your darlings.

Any writing that does not support your thesis and strengthen the document needs to come out, even the clever bits to which you have become overly attached.

"Kill your darlings" is a phrase I learned from Stephen King, so credit for the specific wording goes to him.[8] The general idea is an old one: sometimes there is a bit of brilliant writing—an anecdote, or a clever turn of phrase, or a heartfelt point—that does not advance your thesis. It needs to come out. Your "darling" is not necessarily bad writing; more often, it is a lovely bit of prose that does not fit, like a beautiful sweater that is a size too small. You want it to fit because you like it so much, but it doesn't.

Suppose you are writing a law school admissions essay.

The thesis of the essay is that you are an analytical person with a deep interest in social justice. *You will succeed in law school and the degree will advance your aspirations to make the world a better place.* The essay offers evidence to support this thesis: good grades in law-related classes; internships with social justice organizations; the moving story of your arrest at a climate change protest; and so on. There is also a paragraph about how your Aunt Mabel whispered to you on her deathbed that you should go to law school.

This is a great story, which is why it has survived each round of editing. Mabel was a well-respected schoolteacher whom you admired. The fact that she urged you to go to law school in the final hours of her life is enormously meaningful to you. You love the Mabel story, even as your editing voice tells you that it does not fit with the larger essay. The fact that law school was Mabel's dying wish for you does not support your thesis. It does not explain why you will thrive in law school or what you plan to do with your degree. The Mabel anecdote is your darling. As Stephen King would whisper ominously: *Kill Mabel.*

The law school application example is hypothetical, as is Mabel, but the importance of killing your darlings was brought home to me when I was writing my own graduate school application essay. I was eager to study public policy. I packed my essay with every possible detail that an admissions person could possibly want to know. I was a speechwriter at the time, and I did follow at least some of my own advice (#29). I showed my essay to a fellow speechwriter, Helen. When Helen was done reading the draft, she asked, "Have you ever heard of the Indonesian monkey trap?"

I had not. Helen explained how the Indonesian monkey trap works. Villagers put a banana inside a bamboo cage with vertical slats. The space between the slats is just wide enough for a monkey to slide its hand into the cage and grab the banana. But once the monkey wraps its hand around the banana, the clenched fist no longer fits through the slats. Helen explained to me that the monkeys typically refuse to drop the banana, leaving them trapped.

Then she looked at me and said earnestly, "Sometimes you need to drop the banana." By that, she meant the miscellaneous items packed into my essay that did not make it stronger. I have no idea if there is really such a thing as an Indonesian monkey trap. For the record, I do not endorse the trapping of monkeys. Also, I suspect that monkeys are smart enough to drop the banana. None of these points is important here. I trimmed the essay—*I killed my darlings.* Also, I was accepted into a graduate program, which, if you recall point #1, is why I was writing the essay.

31. In school, the smartest people write the longest papers; in life, the smartest people write the shortest memos.

The best document is one that does everything
it needs to do as succinctly as possible.

Busy people have limited time. The most valuable thing you can offer them is a document that tells them everything they need to know as quickly as possible. What needs to go in? How can it be expressed most succinctly? What can be left out? I have quoted Winston Churchill's memo to his war cabinet repeatedly. Now I will reveal its title: "Brevity." The memo concludes: "Reports drawn up on the lines I propose may at first seem rough as compared with the flat surface of officialese jargon. But the saving in time will be great, while the discipline of setting out the real points concisely will prove an aid to clearer thinking."

I teach a class that requires a final group project. Each group must design an economic plan suitable for a presidential campaign. The proposals must make economic sense, but the assignment is also a writing exercise. Each group must present its economic plan in a clear and compelling way. Moments after I present the assignment, the first hand goes up: "How long should this be?"

I reply, "I'm not going to answer that." This prompts gasps of disbelief. My intent is not to be coy or secretive. The point is to imitate writing for life. When the murmurs of concern have died down, I explain, "Your memo needs to be long enough to explain the content thoroughly, but not so long as to waste my time."

"Well how long is that?" a conscientious student invariably asks.

"A good memo needs to persuade the reader that your policy makes sense," I answer. There are sighs of relief as students conclude that the best way to make a memo persuasive is by packing it with information. Longer must be better. After all, that was true in high school. Then I add, "If the weather is nice, I would much rather be playing golf than reading your overly long memos. So, don't waste my time."

This is when panic sets in. *How long is long enough but not too long?* That is trickier than an assignment specifying eight pages or ten pages or nine hundred and fifty words. Yet after you leave school, rarely will you get a writing assignment with an arbitrary length (unless it is a *maximum* length). You will never hear this conversation in an executive suite:

CEO: Write a letter to our shareholders explaining how we lost $17 billion last year. Also, say that we're sorry for the accounting fraud and that we're working to reduce the number of toxic waste leaks.

AMBITIOUS YOUNG PROFESSIONAL: How long should it be?

CEO: Seven pages, double-spaced.

AMBITIOUS YOUNG PROFESSIONAL: What font size?

CEO: Let's do 12-point type, with one-inch margins.

AMBITIOUS YOUNG PROFESSIONAL: Maybe the Calibri font?

CEO: Yes, I love that font.

Never in the history of corporate America has that conversation taken place. Seven pages with one-inch margins is an arbitrary length offered by fifth-grade teachers assigning reports on butterflies. And that's fine—for fifth grade. The letter to the shareholders must inform, explain, and apologize without blathering on. The length, font, and margins should be whatever produces a letter that most effectively discourages the shareholders from firing the management team. No longer and no shorter.

Some of my students' memos end up too short. I offer feedback such as, "This needs to be explained" or "You need to support this statement with evidence." Others are too long. They get comments like "This section is redundant" or "The memo would be stronger if you cut this whole paragraph." Many are too short in some sections and too long in others.

In middle school, when the smart girl who sat in the front row turned in a report on butterflies that was twice as long as every other student's report, it was likely better, too. She had done more work than the other students, which was signaled to the teacher by the number of pages. Other students marveled at her long report—and also at the attractive hand-colored cover. The guy in the back row who turned in the one-page report was not the class genius.

But when it comes to briefing a CEO or a board chair or a prime minister, the staffer who turns in the one-page report might be the smartest. Long documents take up a disproportionate amount of someone else's time. *Have you earned all those pages? Could you have conveyed the same information more efficiently?* The staff members who write overly long memos are the equivalent of the slackers in the back row. If they were better writers, or if they had taken more time to edit, the memo would have been shorter.

Shorter documents can also be more persuasive. Organizational psychologist Niro Sivanathan has studied something he calls the "dilution effect."[9] When it comes to influence, he argues, quality is more important than quantity. Adding weaker arguments dilutes the impact of the strongest points. Sivanathan conducted an experiment in which one group of study participants was shown an advertisement for a prescription drug that listed all of its side effects, major and minor: heart attack, stroke, and also toenail fungus, bad breath, diarrhea, knee pain, etc. (I do not know the exact side effects they listed; I am making these up for illustrative purposes.) The other study participants saw the ad with only the major side effects: heart attack and stroke. Logic suggests that the first advertisement would be most impactful because it lists more things that may go wrong. Or perhaps both ads would be equally effective since consumers care most about heart attack and stroke and will ignore toe fungus and diarrhea.

In fact, participants who saw the advertisement with all the major and minor side effects rated the drug's potential adverse effects as *less severe* than the participants did who saw the advertisement with only the major side effects.

The minor side effects diluted consumers' overall risk assessment of the drug. When one begins reading about toenail fungus and knee pain, it diverts attention from heart attack and stroke. This is Sivanathan's dilution effect: more arguments are not better; they weaken the case. "Stick to your strong arguments," he advises, "because your arguments don't add up in the minds of the receiver, they average out."

Short speeches pack a punch, too. Civil rights icon John Lewis gave one of the most important speeches at the March on Washington in 1963. Singer and longtime civil rights activist Harry Belafonte was there. He recalls, "John Lewis delivered a kind of Gettysburg Address. It was one of the most brilliant speeches I'd ever heard. He spoke for the young, for the future of America."

How long was John Lewis's speech? *Seven and a half minutes*.[10]

Niro Sivanathan's TED talk on the dilution effect described above—a relatively complex phenomenon—is just under eleven minutes.

Shorter may be better, but it's not necessarily easier. Succinct documents and presentations require discipline, discretion, and many rounds of editing. Hence the aphorism attributed to many different people: "If I had more time, I would have written a shorter letter."

32. Hit your limit.

If you have been given a limit—a word limit, or a
page limit, or a space limit—then observe it.

If someone tells you to show up for an important meeting at 4:15, you don't saunter in at 5:10. Why? Because it is rude and wasteful of someone else's time. The same is true for writing an eight-page memo when your colleague has asked for a one-page summary. The person who gave you a limit presumably had a reason for it. Maybe there is only so much space in the newsletter. Perhaps a Senate candidate will be reading eleven memos on other topics and has only so much time to absorb them all. Maybe the person who asked you to write one page on penguin habitats cares less about penguins than you do. Whatever the reason, show the discipline and respect necessary to achieve the assigned objective in the allotted space.

It does not matter how much space you believe the topic deserves. What matters is how much space you have been given. The reader is the customer. Consider this hypothetical conversation between New England Patriots coach Bill Belichick and quarterback Mac Jones:

COACH BELICHICK: Okay, Mac, there's a minute and fifty-six seconds on the clock. Time for our two-minute drill. Let's move the ball down the field and score.

MAC JONES: Coach, with all due respect, I need four minutes to do everything that I'd like to do here.

COACH BELICHICK: There's only a minute and fifty-six seconds on the clock.

MAC JONES: Yeah, I see that, Coach, but I've got so many interesting plays that I'd like to try—some passes, some runs. Two minutes would really cramp my style.

COACH BELICHICK: Use the time on the clock, or I'm putting in your replacement.

If you have a minute and fifty-six seconds, then make a plan that will take no longer than a minute and fifty-six seconds. In the writing world, that means organizing the material for the space allotted. At the beginning of a project, you are free to negotiate the word or space limit, just as you are free to ask if it would be okay to arrive at 6:30 rather than 6:00 when someone invites you to dinner. But once the limit is established, abide by it.

33. Once you know the rules, you can consider disregarding them.

Strong writers can bend or suspend the rules to good effect.

The rules for good writing are a starting point. Like traffic laws, they have evolved because they produce good outcomes. As with any rules, however, there may be times when it makes sense to dispense with them. There is usually a good reason that the speed limit on a particular road is thirty-five miles per hour. At the same time, you might reasonably choose to drive fifty miles an hour while rushing your pregnant wife to the hospital after she has gone into labor. (This happened to us.) If you are going to disregard a rule, you should understand why the rule exists in the first place and how breaking it will produce a better outcome (e.g., not delivering a baby in the front seat of the car).

Choosing to disregard a rule is different from not knowing the rule in the first place. People who break the rules because they do not know them are bad writers, just as people who are oblivious to traffic laws are bad drivers. In contrast, Shakespeare invented over seventeen hundred words during his career.[11] Words like "eyeball" and "gossip" did not exist in the English language until Shakespeare created them. You, too, should make up your own words—if you are as talented as Shakespeare.

Imagine you are at a banquet with the Queen of England as the guest of honor. As the guests look on, the queen picks up a fried chicken drumstick and begins eating with her hands. This gesture will be perceived as delightful and endearing. Why? Because the queen is better versed on etiquette than nearly everyone in the world. She knows that it is traditionally impolite to eat with one's hands. If she chooses to eat chicken with her hands, she is inviting everyone around her to be more relaxed. The queen is so down to earth! She's just like one of us!

Now consider a different scenario. You have brought your college roommate home for Thanksgiving. At the beginning of the meal, he begins eating the mashed potatoes with his hands. Your family does not say, "He's so down to earth! He's just like one of us!" They are more likely to look on in disgust and ask you later in the kitchen, "Does he know how to use silverware?"

There are plenty of cases where you may choose to do the grammatical equivalent of eating with your hands. The phrase "I think" is usually unnecessary, as noted earlier. If you are saying or writing something, then presumably you are the one thinking it. But the phrase "I think" can also be a mark of humility. If an eloquent person says, "I think it's a good idea," the phrase "I think" softens the statement by implicitly suggesting that others may disagree.

Compare the following:

We should close the school if another student tests positive for Covid.

My sense is that we should close the school if another student tests positive for Covid.

The first statement is stronger and more emphatic. Sometimes that is the tone you are striving for. Yet the second statement might be the right one at a school board meeting where you are seeking to recognize that there is a diversity of defensible opinions.

I began this book with the incongruous sentence, "How lost is he?" My eighth-grade English teacher emphasized repeatedly that some words are binary, such as *round* and *unique*. An object is either round or it's not. One circle cannot be "rounder" than another. Rather, one would say "more nearly round." Similarly, something that is unique means that it is one of a kind. Something is either unique—there is none other like it—or it is not unique. Nothing is "very unique." (If something is unusual but not unique, one might describe it as "nearly unique," or "singular.") Why did I begin a book on writing with a phrase that my eighth-grade English teacher would object to? Because "How lost is he?" was such a beautiful use of language. That was Shakespeare inventing a new word.

Consider a recent headline in my excellent local paper, the *Valley News*: "[Governor] Scott Won't Not Let Pot Be Bought in Vermont." At first glance, this would appear to be a grammatically disastrous headline composed by people who ought to know better. Using a double negative is a basic grammar faux pas. One would never say, "I'm not not going to the supermarket." Rather, we use the clearer and more direct statement, "I am going to the supermarket." Similarly, the sentence, "He doesn't not want to go" is a mess. *He wants to go.*

But let us unpack the double negative in the newspaper headline. In the state of Vermont, the governor has three options after the legislature passes a bill. He can sign the bill, enacting it into law. He can veto the bill, rejecting it unless the legislature overrides the veto. Or, most subtly, he can let a bill become law without his signature. In this case, the governor is not standing in the way of the legislation—there is no veto—but he signals his disapproval by not signing the bill. It's like a parent telling a child, "I don't think you should buy a motorcycle, but I'm not going to stop you."

Now, back to marijuana in Vermont. In 2020, the Vermont legislature passed a bill legalizing the commercial sale of marijuana. The governor, a Republican who had previously opposed marijuana legalization, opted not to exercise his veto, thereby allowing the bill to become a law. But he did not sign it. Which brings us back to the headline: "Scott Won't Not Let Pot Be Bought in Vermont."

The governor is not approving of legalized marijuana in Vermont. But he's not stopping it either. So, what is he doing? He's not stopping it. I suspect the headline writers, always looking for a way to grab attention with a headline (#28) decided to have fun with the double negative—the journalism equivalent of the Queen of England eating chicken with her fingers. On second glance, particularly after you read the story, the headline is a clever, ironic use of grammar.

Language and the rules for using it will evolve, just like traffic laws. (There was no legal right turn on red when I was young; the maximum speed limit everywhere was fifty-five miles per hour.) The word "data" has traditionally been plural: *The data in support of the plan are compelling.* Now the *New York Times* and other authorities have declared that it can be singular: *The data is compelling.* For reasons related to our evolving understanding of gender, the pronoun "they" can now be singular. This healthy process will continue, but nothing about evolving rules absolves you from knowing what they are.

Have fun with language and grammar—but only after you have demonstrated that you are not the rube eating mashed potatoes with your hands.

34. Read good writing. Watch good presentations.

*The best way to get better at anything is to study
the work of people who are good at it.*

Every good piece of writing, from a scintillating *New Yorker* article to a pithy email from the sales manager, offers a potential lesson in writing better. When students turn in policy memos to me, I select a handful of the best and put them on reserve for other students to read. They are a teaching tool.

Why was that introduction so effective? How did this person use graphics and appendices? What kind of evidence did she present to support her case? These memos show how the assignment can be done better. Or, if you want to look at the situation more cynically, it reminds them that I am the customer—the person giving grades—and the customer really liked these memos.

We could all learn something from best-selling writer Robin Cook, who did not start out as a best-selling writer. Cook was a medical student when he wrote his first book. It flopped. He then spent nearly five years studying books that didn't flop, such as *Jaws* and *Love Story*, to learn the techniques for making a book suspenseful and enjoyable. "Between my first book and my second book I attempted to give myself a course in creative writing," Cook explained to an interviewer.[12] Cook's next book, *Coma*, was a huge hit. (I have read it twice, including once when I was teaching myself how to write fiction.) Robin Cook has sold one hundred million books in his long career.

Actor Tom Hanks did something similar when he aspired to become a short story writer. He read "two volumes of the best writing from the *New Yorker*."[13] In 2017, Hanks published *Uncommon Type: Some Stories.*

In business, companies routinely "reverse engineer" competitors' products. They take them apart to understand how and why they work well. If you want to be serious about writing, you need to read the good work of others—and then reverse engineer it.

35. Redefine what it means to be a good writer.

Good writing accomplishes what it was intended to do.

Remember where we began: Good writing begins with *why*. What did you hope to accomplish when you sat down in front of a blank screen or piece of paper? Why are you standing at the front of the room with people looking at you?

The most basic definition of good writing is that it succeeds. With that metric in mind, let us consider two scenarios involving the use of language:

Scenario One: You write a short but compelling email to your boss asking for a 5 percent raise. She replies that your request seems fair and sends a note to human resources telling them to pay you more.

Scenario Two: You send a cover letter to a prospective employer with witty film references, brilliant metaphors, short passages from the *Talmud*, and an inspiring quotation from Gandhi. Most impressive, the whole cover letter is composed in iambic pentameter and printed on paper made from composted food waste. Several days later, you receive a terse email informing you that there are no positions available.

By my reckoning, the first bit of writing was effective and the second one was not. There is a relevant aphorism related to the life of Buddha. According to the story, a man informed Buddha that he had figured out how to walk on water, allowing him to walk across a river from one bank to another. The Buddha replied, "Yes, but the ferry only costs a nickel."

Writing for your life is about getting across the river, not walking on water. You are writing to achieve some objective. Sure, if you are writing poetry in your spare time, the beauty of those words is the objective. More often, you will be clarifying, promising, persuading, entertaining, explaining, complaining, reporting, asking, pleading, apologizing, or otherwise using language to achieve some end.

In researching this book, I checked out a volume of Winston Churchill's war papers from the Dartmouth College library. The volume is nearly thirteen hundred pages long. Churchill is known for his witty style and sardonic humor. Few writers have used the English language more adeptly. But do you know what makes Churchill's war papers truly extraordinary? *They won World War II.*

One hopes that your writing will never be necessary to win a war. There will be some purpose, however. You may be relieving a friend's loneliness, making the case for a constitutional amendment, or urging your local supermarket to carry shelf-stable gnocchi. You will sit at the keyboard or step to the microphone at a town meeting with the expectation that your words will change the world in some way, big or small.

SOME POINTS SPECIFIC TO PRESENTATIONS

Like good writing, speaking in public is an essential life skill. Successful people across a broad range of professions have an ability to express themselves succinctly and articulately. If you expect to be in a position of leadership, whether that is leading a community group or running a company, you must be able to present material to a group in a way that projects competence.

As I have sought to express, effective speaking is identical in many respects to good writing. Your talk presumably has a purpose. You should know what your thesis is. After you have been speaking for thirty seconds or so, your listeners should know what that thesis is, too. You will have an audience, literally, and you should adapt your content and style to that audience. You will need a snappy beginning and a memorable close. In between, there must be an effective narrative structure.

The people listening to your talk must be persuaded that

you are correct. You should use vivid examples, support your assertions with data, and so on. One notable difference between speaking and writing is that listeners have less capacity to absorb numbers than readers do. If you bombard an audience with facts and figures, most of them will bounce off. Stories are a particularly compelling speaking tool because they engage the audience and are likely to stick with them. I will return to this point.

As with writing, if you want to get better at public speaking, you should study good speeches. This has never been easier. TED talks are accessible free online; the best of them are inspiring and fun to watch. (Part of the genius of TED is the eighteen-minute time limit.) I also recommend a wonderful podcast called *It Was Said* in which historian Jon Meacham dissects seminal speeches, such as John Lewis's speech at the March on Washington, Hillary Clinton's Beijing speech on women's rights, Ronald Reagan's farewell address, and Meghan McCain's eulogy for her father, John McCain, former US senator and presidential candidate. Meacham puts each speech in historical context and explains why it was so effective.

To recap, if you want to be an effective speaker, start with the tips for being a good writer. Both writing and speaking require organizing your words to good effect. Of course, speaking has one crucial difference: at some point, you have to say the words out loud in front of other people. Here are some additional suggestions for making that part go well, too.

1. Be prepared from the minute you stand up.

You don't get a second chance to make a first impression, particularly as a public speaker.

What would you think of a presenter who begins his talk by tapping the microphone and saying, "Testing, testing. Is this on?" Perhaps this is followed by loud feedback from the sound system—a horrible, screeching noise—at which point people in the audience begin yelling, "Move the microphone away from the speakers!" Would this make you believe that a great speech is about to happen?

How does that compare to someone who steps to the microphone, looks confidently at the audience, and says, "I want to tell you about a time a man put a gun to my head and asked me whether I wanted to live or die."

There is no feedback from the microphone. No one in the back of the room is yelling, "We can't hear you!" Instead, people are leaning forward in their seats eager to hear the rest of the story.

The beginning of your speech is like the introduction to a written document. You need to succinctly convey what you are going to talk about. One crucial difference with speaking is that those first few seconds also signal to your audience whether you are competent at public speaking or not. Persuade them that you are. You should know before you step to the podium whether the microphone is on. You should know whether people in the back can hear you, either because you've practiced with the sound system, or because you've observed the speakers before you, or because you are paying careful attention to all parts of the room when you begin speaking. Your remarks need not be scripted or memorized, but the beginning of your talk should suggest to your audience that the balance of what you are going to say is worth listening to.

I once attended a rehearsal dinner for a wedding at which a guest stood up to give a toast and said sheepishly, "I really haven't prepared anything."

At that point, Allen Gerstein, an accomplished trial lawyer, said loudly from the audience, "Then sit down."

His assessment still rings true to me.

2. Make sure in advance that your technology will work flawlessly.

The technology you use to support your speech is like a weapon you bring into battle; make sure you can depend on it.

Nothing will interrupt the flow of your presentation and compromise your credibility like a five-minute interruption as three strangers from the audience try to get the projector to work. When one of them says loudly, "Does anyone have a USB-c adapter?" the audience's expectations for your talk will plummet further.

The technology you can use to support your presentations is getting steadily more advanced. You can incorporate videos, play music, take polls of the audience, and so on. But "more advanced" does not necessarily mean easier to use. Complexity invites complications. I have seen presentations where technology vividly enhances the message of the speaker; I have seen at least as many where it becomes a major distraction. When my students do presentations, roughly half are interrupted by some technology-related snafu (often because they are pushing the boundaries of what can be done).

Test your technology ahead of time. You should have a backup plan if that technology fails. What if the Internet goes out? What if the person who is supposed to bring the projector forgets it? I once asked a former pitcher for the New York Yankees how he prepared for a big game. He explained that the night before the game, he envisioned facing every batter in the opposing lineup. He mentally prepared by pitching a whole game—batter by batter—in his mind.

Great performances, and even passably good ones, require excellent preparation.

3. Never read your text unless an errant comment is likely to move markets or bring down a government.

Reading a text makes you a less engaging speaker.

A written text puts distance between the speaker and the audience. Unless you are a well-rehearsed reader (e.g., the president of the United States using a teleprompter), your voice will lose its natural inflections. This will also be true if you have memorized a speech and are reciting it. Your listeners will feel, correctly, that you are speaking at them, not with them. A better alternative in most situations is to become comfortable speaking from a detailed outline. The outline gives structure to your talk and ensures that you will get certain things correct, such as names and figures. At the same time, an outline gives you flexibility to speak conversationally about each point.

If you were making a five-minute pitch to the Planning Board about the need to upgrade the municipal swimming pool, your notes might look like the following:

Introduction: The current swimming pool is decrepit. The necessary upgrades are affordable.
- Story: School group joking about the smell in the locker room.
- Thanks to Planning Board members who were on the exploratory committee:
  ‣ Jim Keane
  ‣ Martha Beattie
  ‣ Leah Yegian
- Estimates for the upgrade work are broadly similar from all three contractors:
  ‣ $1.5 million to renovate locker rooms and deck area
  ‣ $4 million to reline pool, replace the pump, upgrade food service, and reseal the parking lot
- Broad community support:
  ‣ Nonbinding referendum supported pool improvements: 62% in favor.

▸ Pass out column favoring upgrade written by local *Daily
Dispatch* writer Porter Bowman.

▸ Local celebrity Chuckford Pickens has pledged $500k
toward the project.

Finish: Swimming pool is an important community asset
and a source of pride.

• The community supports making the necessary
improvements.

• Story: Chuckford Pickens's apology for peeing in the pool
as a young boy.

The outline will lead you logically through your presentation. It will steer you back on track if you lose your place.
In fact, an outline is more flexible than a written text in this
regard. If you have written out every word and sentence and
you lose your place, you must find the exact spot where you
departed from the text, or the speech will feel disjointed. An
outline directs you back to your next point without the need
for some predetermined transition.

Obviously, some formal events require a prepared text:
commencement addresses, testimony to Congress, remarks
by the chair of the Federal Reserve. These are situations in
which a single errant word can have grave repercussions.
One assumes that if the Soviets had instigated World War III,
the queen would have stuck to the text.

If you are extremely nervous, a written text can be a source
of support. In that case, you should do your best to memorize

the speech, the previous caveat notwithstanding. The more practice you put into your talk, the more conversational it will appear. For most situations, however, speaking from a detailed outline offers a happy medium: it offers the organizational structure of a text and a conversational delivery that is more engaging for the audience.

4. Use graphics (e.g., PowerPoint) as a tool for amplifying or clarifying what you are saying, not as a crutch.

Visual images, including video, can be extremely powerful; text-heavy bullet points are not.

Your audience is there to hear you speak, not to hear you read from a screen that they can see themselves. TED talks, which have become the gold standard for effective presentations, forbid word-heavy slides because they draw attention away from a good speaker. The best graphics are those that complement a talk with an image or images that are uniquely powerful, just like photos in a text.

I often give talks on the need for political reform. In particular, I advocate for ending the practice of gerrymandering, which is when the politicians who control a state legislature draw legislative districts in a way that unfairly advantages their own party. (Here is how I frame it: *Voters should pick their representatives, not the other way around.*) I use the following slide because it demonstrates the shameful degree to which

The Evolution of Maryland's Third District

83rd Congress	88th	93rd	98th
103rd	108th	113th	

I use this slide in presentations on gerrymandering to express visually how gerrymandering has grown worse over time and that the resulting congressional districts make no sense for anyone other than the politicians who design them. And then I toss in the aphorism, "Voters should pick their representatives, not the other way around."

Source: Shapefiles maintained by Jeffrey B. Lewis, Brandon DeVine, Lincoln Pritcher, and Kenneth C. Martis, UCLA. Drawn to scale. Graphic: *Washington Post*. Published May 20, 2014

a particular congressional district in Maryland has been gerrymandered. This is something you must see to believe.

Your graphics should make what you are saying clearer, funnier, or more poignant. If you are trying to explain the emotions soldiers feel when they return from Afghanistan and meet their families for the first time, you might play a short video clip of such a reunion. A great image is one that an audience will remember months or even years later. A good example is this photo of a soldier returning from Vietnam. I went in search of this image because I remembered seeing it as a young boy. I still have an emotional response to it.

The emotional resonance of this image has stuck with me for decades.
Lieutenant Colonel Robert Stirm is reunited with his family upon his
return from Vietnam in 1973. The photo by Associated Press photographer Slava Veder won the Pulitzer Prize for Feature Photography.
AP Photo / Sal Veder.

I once took students to a meeting with an academic who
projected a Microsoft Word document on the screen and spent
the next hour reading aloud from it (as we read along). It
would have been easier for everyone if he had just emailed us
the document. When one of my Dartmouth colleagues began
distributing the slides for his lectures ahead of time, students
stopped coming to the class. Everything he covered in the lectures was in the PowerPoint. That may be fine in some cir-
cumstances, but then skip the talk. What you have produced
is a report, not a presentation.

Slides can work like an outline in helping you organize your talk. When I give presentations on economics, I use a slide with a photo of an overflowing bowl of cashews. That's the only thing on the slide: a picture of a bowl of cashews. It prompts me to tell a particular story about Nobel Prize–winning economist Richard Thaler, just as if I had written "cashew story" in an outline. Thaler's most important economic insight—the one for which he was awarded the Nobel Prize—came to him while he was eating a bowl of cashews with some of his University of Chicago colleagues. (I have put the story in Appendix B.)

Graphics can make your speech better. They can also make it much worse. The key is to design a good talk *without graphics*, and then add images to enhance it, like adding frosting to a cake. If your cake is awful, the frosting will not rescue it. On the other hand, if your cake is delicious, frosting will make it more enticing.

5. Tell stories.

*Telling a relevant story will underscore your point,
engage your listeners, and make you less nervous.*

I have already addressed the power of stories in your writing. I'm going to restate this point because stories are such an important tool for public speaking, too. Most of us are not comfortable recounting facts and figures in front of an audience, but we are natural storytellers. We do it all the time.

"You see this scar above my eye? Let me tell you where it came from."

"The first time I cooked the Thanksgiving meal, it did not go well."

"We were two days from the Colombian border, with the police in close pursuit, when we ran out of water."

From a public-speaking standpoint, stories are elegant because they tend to be self-organizing. They have an inherent narrative structure: Tell the audience what happened in whatever way feels most natural.

How much do I love kale? Well, let me tell you a story about that. I got to the organic produce aisle at the same time as a large man in a leather vest with a skull and crossbones tattooed on his bare bicep. We both stared at the one remaining bunch of organic kale. The man growled at me, "I'm making a kale-and-white-bean soup tonight for six of my biker buddies, and you aren't going to stop me." I could see the can of Great Northern beans in his recyclable shopping bag, so I knew he was serious.

Telling a story will put you at ease as a speaker. I wrote speeches for Chicago mayor Richard Daley when he went on the speaking circuit after serving as mayor for twenty-two years. Let me be honest: Mayor Daley is not a brilliant public speaker. He mumbles. He stumbles over long words. He loses his place in the text and sometimes skips entire pages. *But he is a fantastic storyteller.* The speeches I wrote for him included as many stories as possible. After a paragraph thanking the hosts, I would insert a simple prompt: *Nixon at O'Hare story*. That was sufficient to remind the mayor to tell a funny but meaningful story about the time his father (also a mayor of Chicago) took him to O'Hare Airport to meet President Richard Nixon. Mayor Daley told the story a little differently every time, but it always worked.

Children love stories. They will plead to hear more of them before bedtime. Adults appreciate a good story, too. The irony is that stories are not merely entertainment; as with writing, they are a powerful way to make an important point. Sal Khan, founder of Khan Academy, has given a popular TED talk on mastery learning: the idea that a student should have a complete understanding of any topic before moving on to another topic that demands the same skills. For example, no student can be successful at calculus without mastery of algebra. In his TED talk, Sal Khan offers a story that explains the concept brilliantly while amusing his audience:

In a traditional classroom, you have homework, lecture, homework, lecture, and then you have a snapshot exam. And that exam, whether you get a 70 percent, an 80 percent, a 90 percent or a 95 percent, the class moves on to the next topic. And even that 95 percent student—what was the five percent they didn't know? Maybe they didn't know what happens when you raise something to the zeroth power. Then you build on that in the next concept. That's analogous to—imagine learning to ride a bicycle. Maybe I give you a lecture ahead of time, and I give you a bicycle for two weeks, then I come back after two weeks, and say, "Well, let's see. You're having trouble taking left turns. You can't quite stop. You're an 80 percent bicyclist." So I put a big "C" stamp on your forehead—and then I say, "Here's a unicycle."

But as ridiculous as that sounds, that's exactly what's happening in our classrooms right now. And the idea is you fast-forward and good students start failing algebra all of the sudden, and start failing calculus all of the sudden, despite being smart, despite having good teachers, and it's usually because they have these Swiss cheese gaps that kept building throughout their foundation. So our model is: learn math the way you'd learn anything, like riding a bicycle. Stay on that bicycle. Fall off that bicycle. Do it as long as necessary, until you have mastery.[1]

Many speakers begin a speech with a joke. I have seen that fail miserably more often than I have seen it succeed. The humor may offend or fall flat, in which case you have flubbed your first impression. On the other hand, heartfelt stories are a win-win-win: the speaker is comfortable telling them; the audience likes to hear them; and they convey an idea in a memorable way.

6. Be aware of how your audience is responding.

The reactions of the people listening will give you real-time feedback on how you are doing.

No one is going to send you a note at the podium that says, "Hey, you are really boring." Nor will someone stand up in the back and ask, "How much longer do you think you're going to speak?" They will, however, deliver that message indirectly: by looking at their watches, texting under the table, whispering to the person next to them, or doing something else that suggests they are tired of listening to you.

It can be hard to keep the attention of the room. You may be speaking to people early in the morning. You may be speaking to people after dinner when they have had several glasses of wine. You may be speaking at a small meeting with people who are worried about the work they should be getting done. We have all been in a talk or meeting where some poor soul gets the head bobs. His eyes close and his chin drifts down toward his chest, and then suddenly he wakes and his head snaps up. Seconds later, the eyes are half-closed again... Supreme Court Justice Ruth Bader Ginsburg, who served on the court until she died at age eighty-seven, famously fell asleep during Barack Obama's 2015 State of the Union Address (and also during his 2010 address).[2]

Alternatively, your audience may be laughing, or nodding along, or shaking their heads in disagreement (which is

Supreme Court Justice Ruth Bader Ginsburg nods off during the 2015 State of the Union Address. Isn't it fun to see this photo here? See writing suggestion #25, "Insert graphics and photos that support your analysis." AP Photo / Pablo Martínez Monsiváis.

still engagement). A good speaker reads the room, just as a pro quarterback reads the defense. If the audience is getting antsy, you need to adapt with a break, or a story, or something else that will reengage them. If you have the opportunity to give the same talk on more than one occasion, use this listener feedback to make your presentation better: do more of what worked and less of what didn't.

You may also get formal feedback from the audience after your talk. You might, for example, receive some kind of numerical score and/or open-ended comments. This is effectively a grade from your listeners, which can be helpful. But a good speaker does not need to wait days or weeks to get feed-back: just watch the audience.

7. Consider asking questions of the audience, or doing other things to break through the barrier between you and your listeners.

Engage your listeners by making them active participants.

The more passive your audience, the more distant they will feel from your talk. This is especially true with remote pre-sentations (e.g., Zoom), when listeners can literally turn you off. Even in person, the audience will zone out if they do not feel engaged. What is the best way to prevent that? *By making them active participants.*

Technology can help. It's now possible to use phone apps or electronic clickers to poll an audience and present the answers in real time. Low-tech solutions work just as well, such as asking for a show of hands: "How many people got stuck in traffic this morning?" Sometimes you will gather meaningful information. More often, the primary benefit is to transform the audience from passive listeners into people participating in your presentation. When I teach, I use the Socratic method: I ask questions and students answer. Often, I ask really easy questions: "Barack Obama was elected in part because he pledged to expand and reform health care. What year was that?" (2008.) The point of the simple questions is to make it possible for any student to participate. "Before the Affordable Care Act, an insurance company could deny coverage for a preexisting condition. What would be an example of a preexisting condition?" (Type I diabetes.) And so on.

If a particular student appears distracted, I can direct a question to him or her: "Jack, where do Americans over age sixty-five get their health insurance?" (Medicare). This brings Jack back into the conversation while putting everyone else on notice that they might be next. If we have visitors in class, such as a student's parents, I ask them questions, too. "Okay, Kelsey's parents: Do you remember what derailed Gary Hart's campaign?" For a moment, Kelsey's parents look shocked. They had expected to stay hidden in the back row. Now students have turned around and are expecting an answer. After an uncomfortable moment, Kelsey's parents—who are old enough to remember Gary Hart's 1988 presidential campaign—answer the question.* This sends an implicit message to the class: Kelsey's parents are now part of our shared experience.

In a small group, you can ask questions around the table. "Our surgical consultations are down 20 percent this quarter. Priya, are you seeing the same thing in orthopedics?" It is harder to engage a large group, but not impossible. You can ask a question of the audience, for example, and then

---

* Gary Hart was photographed with a woman on his lap who was not his wife. They posed for the picture in front of a boat named *Monkey Business*. His presidential campaign ended shortly thereafter.

invite one person to answer. The point is to break the barrier between you and your listeners. Do not let them treat the talk as if they were sitting on a couch watching television. Passive listeners feel free to turn you off, literally or figuratively. Active listeners won't do that.

An audience of active listeners is a win for everyone. You will have more people paying attention, and those people will enjoy the talk more. The irony of asking a question of Kelsey's parents is that they are excited to be included (once the surprise wears off). Asking them a question transforms them from observers to participants. Do that for all your listeners.

8. Be comfortable with an occasional silence.

There is nothing wrong with taking a moment to compose your thoughts, or to check your notes.

When great speakers pause, the result is a moment of delicious silence as we wait for them to deliver their next thought. These speakers have gravitas. The pause reinforces our impression that they are serious thinkers. In contrast, when a mediocre speaker pauses between thoughts, we get a string of nonsense words: "uh," "umm," "you know." These verbal tics are hard to listen to; they also make the speaker appear less professional.

How can you train yourself to stop saying "uh" and "um"?

By focusing on saying nothing instead. When I taught at the University of Chicago, I videotaped my graduate students giving presentations. Later, we would watch the video together and discuss how the presentation might have been improved. In watching presentations over and over, I learned that students rarely insert an "um" in the middle of a sentence. They use these filler words at transition points as they figure out what to say next. While the brain is searching, the mouth is filling time.

One of the things that makes speaking harder than writing is that we do not have the luxury of going for a walk or making a cup of coffee as we plot our next sentence. All of us need an occasional moment to collect our thoughts. But there is no reason to subject the audience to "uh, hold on, um," as we do it. Just say nothing. Put the mouth in neutral while the brain does its work. These pauses will feel much longer to you than they will to the audience.

There are other words and phrases that are best purged from our speech: *like, actually, literally.* These words do not add meaning or clarity. At best, they detract from the substance of a talk. At worst, they become fabulously annoying. I have a habit of beginning an answer with, "So, ... " I have curtailed that habit (though not broken it entirely) by slowing myself down before I answer. The "so" is a device for buying time as I formulate a thought; now I try to take that time in the form of a pause.

Train yourself not to say things without meaning. It separates those who sound professional from those who do not.

9. Treat the presentation as a conversation with your audience.

Make people feel you are speaking with them, not at them.

When I reviewed the videos of my graduate students' presentations with them, one piece of advice helped more than all others: *Imagine yourself giving this talk at a dinner party.* Suppose you are at the head of the table, and someone asks, "How should we reform our criminal justice system?" How would you answer?*

You would present your thoughts in an organized way, beginning with a statement that summarizes your overall view (e.g., "I think we are incarcerating too many people"). You would make eye contact with your guests, looking around the table. You would speak in a way that did not make your tablemates feel they were being lectured. For example, you might pause on occasion to ask a question. You would use some kind of data or analysis to support your position. You would tell relevant, entertaining stories. You would strive to be engaged with the people you are speaking to, and, if you were succeeding, you would subconsciously notice them leaning in to listen. You would *not* rely on PowerPoint slides.

This "dinner party" advice encapsulates many of the other important recommendations for effective public speaking. My

---

* I'm a policy wonk; the people I hang out with do ask these kinds of questions at dinner parties.

hope is that it will supplant the advice I received about public speaking when I was in high school: *Picture your audience in their underwear.* I'm skeptical of that approach for several reasons. First, I'm not sure it works. Why would imagining people in their underwear make you a more effective speaker? If anything, it would seem to be distracting, depending on the audience. Second, the advice has not aged well. In most places I speak, and certainly on a college campus, if I said, "I'm picturing all of you in your underwear," I would be fired.

To be comfortable in front of an audience big or small, focus on replicating something you have done innumerable times in your life: Speaking naturally to people whom you know well.

10. Know how your talk will end before it just happens to you.

*Make the best of your final opportunity
to persuade the audience.*

Give us a strong finishing thought—something more memorable and effective than, "I guess that's about it." The conclusion of your talk is an opportunity to remind listeners of what your key points were and why they should care about them. Hence, the old aphorism for presentations: *Tell them what you are going to tell them. Tell them. And then tell them what you just told them.* In the language of this book, that would be: Introduce your thesis. Support your thesis. And then remind us of your thesis.

Angela Duckworth is a researcher whose work focuses on the importance of resilience, or "grit." Her excellent TED talk makes the case that while we've been busy using test scores to measure aptitude, we've been missing what really matters, which is a willingness to stick with some task and get better at it, whether that is learning fractions or selling software. This "growth mindset" is crucial to success because it reinforces the idea that ability is not fixed; it can improve with effort.

Here is the finish to Angela Duckworth's TED talk:

Growth mindset is a great idea for building grit. But we need more. And that's where I'm going to end my remarks, because that's where we are. That's the work that stands before us. We need to take our best ideas, our strongest intuitions, and we need to test them. We need to measure whether we've been successful, and we have to be willing to fail, to be wrong, to start over again with lessons learned.

In other words, we need to be gritty about getting our kids grittier.[3]

She reminds us what grit is and why it matters. The last sentence is particularly clever—and a long way from "I guess that's about it."

11. Practice.

This is the equivalent of doing many drafts.

Most people are uncomfortable speaking in public because they don't do it very often. I would be nervous and uncomfortable if I were asked to dance the tango in public. Let us all hope that does not happen. But if it did, I would try to get better at the tango, and the best way to get better at anything is by practicing. The reason many leaders are proficient in public speaking is that they do it over and over again. True, some people have more natural talent than others. But you've just read about grit! The late John Lewis, the civil rights leader and longtime congressman who gave the speech at the March on Washington, learned to preach (and overcome a stutter) by giving sermons to his family's chickens. President Joe Biden also worked tirelessly to overcome a stutter.

You will become more comfortable with public speaking as you do it more frequently. You will get a sense of your own style. You will develop techniques for making yourself less nervous. In the same vein, you should practice any given talk before you give it. This will achieve several things. First, you'll get a sense of how long your talk is, so you can adapt accordingly. Second, you can determine if the narrative structure works. Finally, you will become more comfortable with the material so that it sounds more natural when you deliver it.

Similarly, if you are giving the same talk repeatedly, such as a pitch to investors or a campaign stump speech, you will learn which stories resonate, what graphics best complement your presentation, how you can adapt the talk to the time available, and so on.

In 2009, President Barack Obama tapped Treasury Secretary Tim Geithner to explain the administration's strategy for dealing with the financial crisis. Secretary Geithner's job, according to Obama, was to reassure the country and send "a signal that despite the uncertainty of the times, we were calm and had a credible plan."[4] How did Geithner do? The stock market dropped more than 3 percent *while he was speaking.* Financial stocks fell 11 percent by the end of the day. President Obama would later write, "By every estimation, including [Geithner's] own, the speech was a disaster."

What went wrong? Two things. First, the speech was written by committee. The myriad administration members urging Geithner to emphasize different policies and messages had apparently not read writing tip #13. "The result was a classic speech by committee, full of hedged bets and mixed messages, reflecting all the contradictory pressures," Obama recalls.

Worse, Geithner didn't practice enough, particularly speaking from a teleprompter. Former President Obama notes in his memoir, "In the rush to get it finished, Tim—who was running on fumes at this point—had devoted almost no time to practicing his delivery." The point of the speech was to reassure the country, calm the financial markets, and present the image of an administration in control of the crisis. Geithner's nervous, uncertain presentation had the opposite effect.

Contrary to the old aphorism, practice does not make perfect. But it does make for a lot of improvement. The more often you give a talk, the more familiar you will become with the material, and the more natural your delivery will sound. More broadly, if you want to get better at public speaking, do more of it.

12. Very few speeches in the history of human civilization have been too short.

A great speech accomplishes its objectives as succinctly as possible; if you have been given a time limit, observe it.

Let's talk for a moment about the featured speaker at Gettysburg on November 19, 1863. The event was scheduled to dedicate a military cemetery there. The main speaker that day was Edward Everett, not Abraham Lincoln. Everett had been a US representative, a senator, a governor, a minister to Britain, and the president of Harvard. He was also a renowned speaker. Everett's oration that day lasted roughly two hours.

Abraham Lincoln spoke for less than three minutes. With the benefit of history, we know whose remarks had a more lasting effect. To his credit, Edward Everett recognized in the moment that Lincoln's remarks were brilliantly brief and clear. He wrote the president a note the next day: "I should be glad if I could flatter myself that I came as near to the central idea of the occasion, in two hours, as you did in two minutes."[5] The genius of Lincoln's Gettysburg Address was its clear, powerful message. More words would have only diluted it.

If you have been given a time limit, stick to it. Running over your allotted time is a sign that you have organized your talk poorly. A ten-minute talk should not mean trying to pack thirty minutes of material into the allotted time by speaking quickly, rushing through slides, or simply ignoring the time limit. A ten-minute talk means carefully choosing what you will say and planning for it to fit comfortably into the allotted time.

Running overtime is also rude. If you speak longer than planned, others will have less time to speak, or the audience will have to stay longer than planned. You have become the equivalent of a patient who shows up at the dentist's office fifteen minutes late for the first appointment of the day. Now everyone else on the schedule has to wait because of you.

Finally, running overtime can be torturous for your audience. There are few professional experiences worse than listening to a talk that feels like it might go on forever. When speakers stick to their assigned time limits, the audience knows exactly when a horribly boring speech will come to a close. It's like serving a prison sentence. If the maximum term is eight years, then (assuming good behavior), you'll be out in eight years. But once someone disregards a time limit, we have no idea how long the rambling might continue. At this point, the speaker has signaled poor organization and a disregard for the audience's time.

Keep track of time as you go along. It is never a good sign when the speaker looks up at the clock and says, "Oh my goodness, I'm not going to get through all of this." If the allotted time is twenty minutes, you should be half done at the ten-minute point. If not, you need to adapt.

Bill Clinton, then governor of Arkansas, was a keynote speaker at the 1988 Democratic National Convention. He was invited to speak for fifteen minutes. He spoke for more than half an hour. As his long-winded speech dragged on, there were boos and chants, all the more remarkable because it was a friendly audience. One reporter told listeners while Clinton was speaking, "I can tell you that this place is just ready to explode, and I think they are long past the period of listening to Governor Clinton. [His speech] has gone on so long that he has completely lost this crowd."[6] Clinton did eventually draw rousing applause. It was when he said, "In conclusion . . . "

Don't be that speaker.

13. Decide if you want to take questions, and if so, how you will take them.

Q &A is a nice way to interact with the audience and flesh out the details of your talk; it also opens the door to having the discussion hijacked by long-winded, irrelevant, or hostile questions.

As long as you are at the front of the room speaking, you are in control of the presentation. Once the hands go up and you call on someone (or the moderator does), anything can happen. That may be a good thing. If you are hosting a town hall to make the case for building a new municipal swimming pool, you might choose to listen to all questions that come your way, even the long, hostile ones. The longer you listen to questions and answer them, the more credibility you will have with the public. Everyone will feel listened to.

In other contexts, rambling or irrelevant questions will not make for a great finish to your presentation. It is possible—and I have seen this happen—that a person will step to the microphone after your talk on political reform and complain that fluoridation in the town drinking water is causing cancer. As the presenter, you must navigate the tradeoff between losing control of the discussion and appearing uninterested in getting feedback from all. Technology offers some elegant solutions. You can have audience members submit questions via Twitter or another electronic platform. This allows the speaker or moderator to address the best or most commonly asked questions and skip the crazy ones. Zoom has an "upvote" feature that allows audience members to see questions that have been asked by others and vote for those that they would like to see answered. The questions with the most audience support rise to the top of the screen.

There is a low-tech way to do the same thing: ask audience members to write questions on a notecard and pass them to the front of the room. I once moderated a discussion at Dartmouth's Rockefeller Center with Alex Azar, who at the time was secretary of health and human services in the Trump administration. Secretary Azar is a bright guy with lots of interesting things to say about health care. Yet we were on a college campus and the Trump administration was extremely unpopular. Our goal for the event was to create a forum in which students could engage in a dialogue with Secretary Azar without using the Q & A to shout inappropriate or unconstructive things at him. So, we used the notecard technique.

We passed notecards to all audience members at the beginning of the event. Student volunteers collected the notecards at the end of Secretary Azar's talk and delivered them to me at the front of the room. I flipped through the cards and selected questions. This system had several advantages. First, I could discard questions like "HOW MUCH DID THE DEVIL PAY YOU FOR YOUR SOUL?!!!" Second, I could prioritize questions that were most popular. Many students asked a variation of the same question about reducing the rate of growth in health care spending. I was able to summarize this question and have Secretary Azar address a subject that was of interest to a lot of people. Last, I was able to rephrase questions to make them more succinct, or less gratuitously hostile, while still preserving the essence of a hard question.[*] We achieved what a good Q & A is supposed to achieve: our audience had a chance to engage with the speaker, who answered the most frequent and most interesting questions.

The nature of your talk should determine if and how you want to take questions. How much time do you have? Is the Q & A session meant to be a short period to clarify your talk? Or is it an opportunity for anyone to be heard? Is the audience likely to be supportive or hostile?

Once again, form follows function.

---

[*] Regardless of how you take questions, repeating the question for the audience is a good habit. This does two things. First, it is a courtesy for those who might not have heard the question. In a large room, that may be a high proportion of the audience. Second, it gives you a chance to restate the question more clearly or succinctly. Finally, it gives you a little more time to think about the answer.

CONCLUDING
THOUGHTS

That's about it. I can't really think of anything I haven't covered.

No, I'm not going to finish that way! Have you been paying any attention at all? I'm going to conclude with a story about one of the best writing jobs I ever had. By "best," I mean most enjoyable and most instructive. I was a summer intern in Kuwait in 1987 at an English-language newspaper called the *Arab Times*. (To get the job, I had to sell my motorcycle and use the money to buy an airline ticket to Kuwait, but that's a story for another time.) One of my responsibilities at the *Arab Times* was to write the photo captions for our daily photo page. Every day, the Reuters news service sent us a batch of photos electronically from around the world—everything from war footage to cute animals. My job was to pick ten or twelve of those photos, lay them out on a single page, and write a caption for each.

This was a time-sensitive job. The photos came over the wire late in the afternoon. I had about forty-five minutes to write the captions and deliver them to the typesetters down in the bowels of the building. I did not have a word processor or a computer, just an electric typewriter. Because these photos ran without accompanying stories, the captions had to tell the readers everything they needed to know: the what, where, when, why, and how of each picture. I could use one sentence, or sometimes two, but if the captions got overly long, the photos and captions would not fit on the page. Also, the point of our daily photo page was to offer readers a glimpse of things happening in the world, not paragraphs of analysis.

I sat down every evening and put a sheet of paper in the electric typewriter. Since I was using a typewriter, I had to formulate a complete thought before I began banging away at the keys. On the other hand, I did not have the luxury of staring at the blank page for long. I wrote a cogent caption for each photo. Some were funny (though my snarky text to accompany a photo of the sinister-looking Panamanian dictator Manuel Noriega—"Would you buy a used car from this guy?"—was rejected by the editor). Many were serious. Some were literal and simple: "A polar bear cools off in the water at a Berlin zoo." Each caption told the readers what they needed to know as succinctly as possible. In other words, they did what they had to do, no more and no less. Each day's caption writing made me better, like pushups for writing. Also, those captions have always informed how I think about good writing:

Figure out what kind of writing is necessary for the task at hand.

Do that as succinctly as possible.

Get it to the typesetters by the time they need it (literally or figuratively).

Evaluate success relative to what you set out to accomplish.

Practice if you expect to get better.

That is how you write for your life.

Seriously, would you buy a used car from this guy? Bettmann via Getty Images.

Appendix A

CHURCHILL'S MEMO ON WRITING MEMOS[1]

Winston S. Churchill:
War Cabinet memorandum

(Churchill papers, 23/4)

9 August 1940   10 Downing Street

BREVITY

Memorandum by the Prime Minister

To do our work, we all have to read a mass of papers. Nearly all of them are far too long. This wastes time, while energy has to be spent in looking for the essential points.

I ask my colleagues and their staffs to see to it that their Reports are shorter.

(i)   The aim should be Reports which set out the main points in a series of short, crisp paragraphs.

(ii) If a Report relies on detailed analysis of some complicated factors, or on statistics, these should be set out in an Appendix.

(iii) Often the occasion is best met by submitting not a full-dress Report, but an *Aide-mémoire* consisting of headings only, which can be expanded orally if needed.

(iv) Let us have an end of such phrases as these: 'It is also of importance to bear in mind the following consid-erations . . .', or 'Consideration should be given to the possibility of carrying into effect . . .'. Most of these woolly phrases are mere padding, which can be left out altogether, or replaced by a single word. Let us not shrink from using the short expressive phase, even if it is conversational.

Reports drawn up on the lines I propose may at first seem rough as compared with the flat surface of officialese jargon. But the saving in time will be great, while the discipline of set-ting out the real points concisely will prove an aid to clearer thinking.

WSC

Appendix B

THE CASHEW STORY[1]

University of Chicago economist Richard Thaler was awarded the Nobel Prize in 2017 "for his contributions to behavioral economics." This subfield challenges the traditional economic assumption that humans act consistently in ways that make themselves better off. We're not that rational, it turns out. Richard Thaler's research in this field—the work that would earn him the Nobel Prize—was inspired by a bowl of cashews.

Thaler hosted a dinner party years ago at which he served a bowl of cashews before the meal. He noticed that his guests were wolfing down the nuts at such a pace that they would likely spoil their appetite for dinner. So Thaler took the bowl of nuts away, at which point his guests thanked him. Believe it or not, this little vignette exposed a fault in the basic tenets of microeconomics: In theory, it should never be possible to make rational individuals better off by denying them some option. People who don't want to eat too many cashews before dinner should just stop eating cashews. But they don't. And that finding turned out to have implications far beyond salted nuts.

For example, if humans lack the self-discipline to do things that they know will make themselves better off in the long run (e.g., lose weight, stop smoking, or save for retirement), then society could conceivably make them better off by helping (or coercing) them to do things they otherwise would not or could not do—the public policy equivalent of taking the cashew bowl away. The field of behavioral economics has evolved as a marriage between psychology and economics that offers sophisticated insight into how humans really make decisions.

Acknowledgments

Writing this book was an act of hubris. It screams out, "Hey, I'm good at writing!" The fact is that I have been remarkably lucky to have teachers and editors who got me to a point where I can write things that people are eager to read.

My longtime editor at W. W. Norton, Drake McFeely, is one of those people. This project was bittersweet in that Drake retired just as I was getting started. We were a great team for twenty years, and I enjoyed his coaching and companionship. Drake and I produced a lot of good books together, all of which were better for his prodding and encouragement.

Fortunately, W. W. Norton has a deep bench, and I was lucky to have Matt Weiland and Huneeya Siddiqui take on this project. They are the ones who helped transform a vague idea—*let's help people write better in real life*—into what I hope will be a useful book.

As a professor married to an elementary school principal, I believe that good teaching matters. The recipe for becoming a proficient writer is straightforward: read good books and write as much as possible. I had many teachers who demanded this of me from a young age, but several stand out.

Mrs. Byrne (whose first name I never knew) required her students to read twenty-four books during the academic year and write reports on each of them. We were also expected to know every vocabulary word in everything we read. *That was in fourth grade.*

Bert Satovitz taught sixth grade (by which time I realized that teachers have first names). He was the first to prompt me to think about writing for an audience. He offered feedback on everything we wrote, but he also read our stories aloud to the class. I still remember a story I wrote about President Jimmy Carter that was narrated by one of the lice living on his head: Larry the Louse. The story was a real crowd-pleaser (among sixth graders).

Dorothy Thompson taught eighth-grade language arts twice a day: grammar in the morning and composition in the afternoon. We called Mrs. Thompson "Sarge" behind her back because we'd heard a rumor that she had been an army drill sergeant. Whether Sarge served in the armed forces or not, she tolerated no grammar mistakes. When one of my classmates used the word "kid" colloquially in class, Mrs. Thompson barked, "I don't see a baby goat! Do you? Where's the goat?"

Ken Mularski taught our high school Advanced Placement English class. (We called him "Ken" because by then we were fixated on our teachers' first names.) Obviously, we read great literature, but Ken also persuaded us that we had worthwhile things to say in our own writing. He required us to keep a journal, which is something that I still do nearly forty years later.

For all that, it's a big leap from writing school essays to making a living with a keyboard. Jay Heinrichs, former editor of the *Dartmouth Alumni Magazine,* was the first person to pay me to write something. He considered it his job to cultivate eager young writers, and he was very good at it. The *Valley News,* an excellent local newspaper for a handful of communities in New Hampshire and Vermont, made me a "traveling foreign correspondent" (fifty dollars per story) after I graduated from Dartmouth College. It was exactly the kind of break that an aspiring journalist needs.

Ann Wroe hired me as a correspondent for *The Economist* and made me into a writer worthy of that publication. She and the other excellent editors routinely turned my nine-hundred-word stories into eight-hundred-word pieces that were better for their deft touch.

I owe a debt of gratitude to Dartmouth College for many reasons, but two stand out. First, it is my professional home. I have the privilege of teaching interesting things to engaged students. Dartmouth is also the place I arrived in the fall of 1984 and took an inspiring first-year seminar on short stories. I still love short stories. I have even published a few.

I want to offer special thanks to Tina Bennett, with whom I worked to bring so many different projects to fruition over the years.

Leah is my life editor and makes everything better.

Notes

Introduction: How Lost Is He?

1. Dave Girouard, "A Founder's Guide to Writing Well," https://firstround
.com/review/a-founders-guide-to-writing-well/.
2. David Brooks, "In Her Own Words," *New York Times*, October 13, 2005.
3. Jeffrey Rosen, "Strong Opinions," *New Republic*, July 28, 2011.
4. Rosen, "Strong Opinions."
5. Mark Joseph Stern, "Supreme Court Fish Case: Alito Saves the Day,
Kagan Cites Dr. Seuss," *Slate*, February 25, 2015.
6. Rosen, "Strong Opinions."
7. The Northern Ireland examples were compiled by a group of Dartmouth students in a class on the Northern Ireland peace process. David
Brooks et al., "Insights from Peace and Reconciliation in Northern Ireland," Task Force Report, Fall 2014, 49, https://rockefeller.dartmouth
.edu/sites/rockefeller.drupalmulti-prod.dartmouth.edu/files/pbpl85_
ireland_2014.pdf.
8. "Letter from Birmingham Jail," April 16, 1963, *Martin Luther King, Jr.
Encyclopedia*, Stanford Martin Luther King, Jr. Research and
Education Institute, https://kinginstitute.stanford.edu/encyclopedia/
letter-birmingham-jail.

9. Remarks of First Lady Hillary Rodham Clinton at the Fourth Women's Conference in Beijing, China, September 5, 1995, https://www.youtube.com/watch?v=xXM4E23Efvk.

10. Shaun Usher, *Speeches of Note: An Eclectic Collection of Orations Deserving of a Wider Audience*, New York: Ten Speed Press, 2018.

Writing for Life I: Getting Started

1. Jon Meacham, "Hillary Clinton, Women's Rights Are Human Rights," *It Was Said* podcast, October 14, 2020.

2. Hillary Rodham Clinton, "Women's Rights are Human Rights," Remarks of First Lady Hillary Rodham Clinton, https://www.americanrhetoric.com/top100speechesall.html.

3. Meacham, "Hillary Clinton, Women's Rights."

4. Margaret Talbot, "Is the Supreme Court's Fate in Elena Kagan's Hands?" *New Yorker*, November 11, 2019.

5. *The Economist Style Guide*, Eighth Edition, London: Profile Books, 2003, 1.

6. Jonathan Haidt, *The Righteous Mind: Why Good People Are Divided by Politics and Religion*, New York: Vintage Books, 2012, xxi.

7. "The Persuaders," *Dateline*, November 9, 2004, https://www.pbs.org/wgbh/frontline/film/showspersuaders/.

8. *The Chicago Manual of Style*, 15th Edition, Chicago: University of Chicago Press, 2003.

9. Jon Meacham, "MLK Jr., The Last Speech," *It Was Said* podcast, Episode 1, September 2, 2020.

10. David Kirkpatrick, "Historian Says Borrowing Was Wider Than Known," *New York Times*, February 23, 2002.

Writing for Life II: Making It Better

1. Andrea Elliott, "Invisible Child," *New York Times*, December 9, 2013.

2. "Strait Shooting," *The Economist*, October 10, 2020.

3. Susan Cain, TED Talk, February 2012, https://www.ted.com/talks/ susan_cain_the_power_of_introverts?language=en.

4. Eugene Y. Chan and Sam J. Maglio, "The Voice of Cognition: Active and Passive Voice Influence Distance and Construal," *Personality and Social Psychology Bulletin* 2020, Vol. 46(4): 547–58.

5. Wallace Foundation, *The School Principal as Leader: Guiding Schools to Better Teaching and Learning*, January 2013, https://www.wallacefoundation .org/knowledge-center/Documents/The-School-Principal-as-Leader -Guiding-Schools-to-Better-Teaching-and-Learning-2nd-Ed.pdf.

6. "Not Quite All There," *The Economist*, May 2, 2020.

7. David Goldhill, "How American Health Care Killed My Father," *The Atlantic*, September 2009.

8. Adam Gopnik, "What Makes the Difference Between Getting Out of Prison and Staying Out?" *New Yorker*, November 9, 2020.

9. Nick Paumgarten, "The King of New York," *New Yorker*, October 19, 2020.

10. Marshall Frady, "Death in Arkansas," *New Yorker*, February 22, 1993.

11. Foreword by Robert M. Gates, in Andrew Carroll, *Banner*, produced in 2020 for the political group With Honor.

12. Nelson Mandela, *Long Walk to Freedom: The Autobiography of Nelson Mandela*, Randburg, South Africa: MacDonald Purnell, 1994, 617.

13. Jacob Shelton, "18 Photos of Makeup-Wearing Male Celebs Without Their Makeup On," Ranker, January 24, 2020, https://www.ranker.com/ list/male-celebrities-without-makeup/jacob-shelton.

14. Penny Goldstone, "This Is What It Takes to Get a Celebrity Red Carpet Ready," *Marie Claire*, June 1, 2017.

15. Margaret Talbot, "Is the Supreme Court's Fate in Elena Kagan's Hands?" *New Yorker*, November 11, 2019.

Writing for Life III: Buffing and Polishing

1. Maggie Astor, "A Photo That Changed the Course of the Vietnam War," *New York Times*, February 1, 2018.

2. https://creativecommons.org/publicdomain/zero/1.0/.

Notes

3. Sarah Mervosh, "The Pandemic Ruined Third Grade. Can Summer School Make Up for It?" *New York Times*, July 25, 2021.

4. Barack Obama, *A Promised Land*, New York: Crown, 399.

5. "'It Was Just Thrilling': 2 NPR Founders Remember the First Days, 50 Years Ago," *All Things Considered*, April 28, 2021, https://www.npr.org/transcripts/991268881.

6. George Shultz, "The 10 Most Important Things I've Learned about Trust Over my 100 Years," *Washington Post*, December 11, 2020.

7. "Gambling on the Future," *The Economist*, June 24, 1999.

8. Stephen King (*On Writing: A Memoir of the Craft*, Scribner, 2010) may have gotten it from someone else. In the 1916 book *On the Art of Writing*, Arthur Quiller-Couch advised his readers to "Murder their darlings." Larry Doyle, "Kill Your Darlings," *New Yorker*, February 15 & 22, 2021.

9. Niro Sivanathan on the counterintuitive way to be more persuasive, https://www.ted.com/talks/niro_sivanathan_the_counterintuitive_way_to_be_more_persuasive/transcript?rid=yUpIVdq3A3QI&utm_source=recommendation&utm_medium=email&utm_campaign=explore&utm_term=watchNow#t-$20019.

10. Jon Meacham, "John Lewis, We Want Our Freedom Now," *It Was Said* podcast, Episode 9, October 21, 2020.

11. "Shakespeare's Words," Shakespeare Birthplace Trust, https://www.shakespeare.org.uk/explore-shakespeare/shakespedia/shakespeares-words/#:~:text=William%20Shakespeare%20is%20credited%20with,still%20used%20in%20English%20today.

12. Belinda Goldsmith, "Author Robin Cook Uses Thrillers to Explain Medicine," Reuters Life!, 2020, https://www.reuters.com/article/us-books-authors-cook/author-robin-cook-uses-thrillers-to-explain-medicine-idUKTRE67A1Q820100811.

13. Kate Samuelson, "How Tom Hanks the Movie Star Became Tom Hanks the Short Story Writer," *Time*, November 3, 2017.

Speaking for Life: Some Points Specific to Presentations

1. Salman Khan talks about creating the remarkable Khan Academy, https://www.ted.com/talks/sal_khan_let_s_use_video_to_reinvent_education?language=en.

2. Kendall Breitman, "Ginsburg: I Wasn't '100 Percent Sober' at SOTU," February 13, 2015, https://www.politico.com/story/2015/02/ruth-bader-ginsburg-napping-alcohol-sotu-115172.

3. Angela Lee Duckworth, "Grit: The Power of Passion and Perseverance," TED Talk, April 2013, https://www.ted.com/talks/angela_lee_duckworth_grit_the_power_of_passion_and_perseverance?language=en.

4. Obama, *A Promised Land*, 282.

5. Bob Greene, "The Forgotten Gettysburg Addresser," *Wall Street Journal*, June 22/23, 2013.

6. Tara Golshan, "Bill Clinton's First Major Appearance at a Convention Almost Destroyed His Career," *Vox*, July 26, 2016.

Appendix A: Churchill's Memo on Writing Memos

1. Churchill Archives Centre, The Churchill Papers, CHAR 23/4/4.

Appendix B: The Cashew Story

1. This appendix is adapted from my book *Naked Economics*.

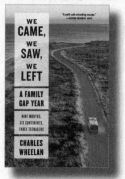